This book is for any
suffered any kind of
small. In other words, for (almost) everyone.

If you ever experienced doubts about the famous
joys of sex, these true stories will prove that,
however bad it was, it could have been worse . . .

Introducing
THE MOST CELEBRATED PROFESSIONAL VIRGIN

THE WORST CASE OF SATURDAY NIGHT FEVER

THE LEAST SUCCESSFUL KNEE-TREMBLER

THE MOST OFTEN DISAPPOINTED SUPERGROUPIE

THE WORST NEWS FOR FLAT-CHESTED
AIR STEWARDESSES

THE MOST INCORRIGIBLE MP

THE LEAST POPULAR SPANKER

THE MOST CONCLUSIVE PROOF THAT
BLONDES DON'T HAVE MORE FUN

THE WETTEST FETISH

THE MOST RAMPANT PENSIONER

– and many more irresistibly awful sexual flops.

PETER KINNELL

The Book of Erotic Failures

Illustrated by Pete Beard

Futura
Macdonald & Co
London & Sydney

A Futura Book

First published in Great Britain in 1984
by Futura Publications, a Division of
Macdonald & Co (Publishers) Ltd
London & Sydney

ISBN 0 7088 2550 8

Typeset, printed and bound in Great Britain by
Hazell Watson & Viney Limited,
Member of the BPCC Group,
Aylesbury, Bucks

Futura Publications
A Division of
Macdonald & Co (Publishers) Ltd
Maxwell House
74 Worship Street
London EC2A 2EN
A BPCC plc Company

ACKNOWLEDGEMENTS

I am particularly indebted to Jenny Prior for the
enormous amount of help she gave me in researching
this book.

Thanks also to Harry Cox and David Evans at the
Daily Mirror Reference Library, *Forum Magazine*, the
British Library, the Colindale Library, the London
Library and the Kensington and Chelsea Library.

CONTENTS

CONTENTS

INTRODUCTION

One of the very few facts to elude the compilers of *The Guinness Book of Records* up to now is the astonishing frequency of erotic failure in men and woman all around the world. For instance, in the time it took you to read that sentence, it is absolutely certain that someone somewhere suffered from an extremely unfortunate and totally humiliating sexual experience.

The reason why this sobering fact has not so far been recorded by the statisticians is hardly surprising. Very few people will own up to being a shambles between the sheets.

Anything else and it's total honesty. 'Of course, I'm a *disaster* when it comes to money/relationships/the new technology,' they'll say proudly. But how many people are there around who will say something like, 'Of course, my problem is that I'm a *terrible* premature ejaculator'? Not many.

Luckily there have been a number of erotic failures around the world that have been so spectacular and embarrassing that sadistic reporters and historians have gleefully recorded them. This book is a collection of some of those champion sexual flops.

Although *The Book of Erotic Failures* can't hope to be comprehensive over such a vast subject, it should at least provide variety in the failures it records, proving that, however many new erotic pleasures are discovered, they are always going to be outnumbered by the pitfalls.

This is not an élitist book. I have not been dazzled by the claims of the great names of history and today, although some (see *Clumsiest Contender, Bunnies Worst*

Buck and *Most Over-Publicized Victorian Gooseberry*, etc) are too gloriously inept to miss.

But on the whole I have found it more interesting to include the unsung casualties of the sex war rather than the fallen generals. We all know that Attila the Hun died on the job, but how many people know what Father Bob Champain was doing with his Bumper Tool Kit at Steynings' Male and Female Lavatory Block? And which is the more socially relevant today?

The people represented in these pages have little in common with one another (in fact, some of them have little in common with anyone), but their vain efforts to achieve sexual satisfaction can teach sexologists of the future some important lessons.

1. *It's always the woman's fault.*

At last, here is the scientific evidence to support what some of the best male brains in history have suspected: that while mankind was going about his business in a red-bloodedly corrupt, randy and perverse way, womankind was relentlessly undermining and humiliating him by being even more corrupt, randy and perverse – only making less fuss about it. How they came to be called 'the fair sex' is a mystery, since sex with a woman is never fair.

2. *The British are not the worst lovers in the world.*

It has been fashionable for foreigners, particularly Americans, to sneer at the way the British make love and suggest that we're not terribly good at it. But while we admittedly have our fair share of erotic failures, they are incomparably more stylish than the messy and undignified disasters that happen abroad. Research shows that the Americans are second only to the Italians in the sexual incompetence stakes.

10

3. *The more famous you become, the worse you are in bed.*

Many of us have experienced that disconcerting moment when we first see a familiar television or film personality in the flesh. 'My goodness,' we think. 'Isn't he *small*?' Those who have been to bed with the stars have almost always reacted in the same way and usually with precisely the same words. The evidence provided here suggests that there is now an urgent need for a study into the connection between fame and sexual failure. These people need help.

If any particularly self-abasing reader (see THE NICEST VICES) feels that he or she could have done worse than these erotic failures, then I must offer my sincere apologies and condolences.

For the rest, I hope that these cautionary tales will reassure those who thought *they* had problems and, at the very least, will prove that Woody Allen just could not have been more wrong when he said, 'Even bad sex is good'.

Peter Kinnell, 1984

ONE

SONGS OF INNOCENCE

'Love of women has always been for me a purifying act of devotion . . . prompted by my love for my mother and vague feelings within'

Hermann Hesse

PUREST NATIONAL SERVICEMAN

It was after a wife complained to her doctor that her husband had never made love to her that his unusual sexual history emerged.

Soon after he was called up for national service, the man had to have a hernia operation, after which the surgeon impressed upon him the need to avoid strenuous exercise at all costs. His friends kidded him that to make love in his condition would have the direst consequences. Terrified at the thought that sex would put him back in hospital, he had remained celibate ever since.

That was twenty years ago.

MOST PATHETIC SEX OFFENCE

In 1975, Mr David Philips, a seventy-seven year old man from Cardiff, was fined £5 for forty-two kiss-and-run incidents involving female traffic wardens.

SHYEST NEWLYWEDS

A young couple in Huntingdon suffered an unfortunate start to married life, according to a report in the *Journal of Sexual Medicine*.

Rosemary and Alan were both seventeen and virgins

when they got married. Two years later, they had been unable to get any privacy to take the plunge.

At first, the problem had been the fact that they were living with Rosemary's parents. Then, when they were given her grandparents' house, it was on condition that they kept the ancient lodger who lived there. They were convinced that he would hear them too.

In agonies of embarrassment, they went to a sex counselling clinic. After six months they had overcome their anxiety enough to try to make love.

'But at the critical moment,' the journal reports, 'the lodger screamed and collapsed and died.'

MOST ELABORATE SALES CAMPAIGN

Sexual anxiety ran riot in the streets of Donala, Cameroon, when a number of young men claimed to have become impotent after a stranger had put the 'evil eye' on them.

One man dropped his trousers in the middle of a busy street and invited passers by to witness the fact that he had lost his sexual powers. Panic-stricken that the condition was contagious, all around the desperate flasher fled for cover.

Soon men all over the town were claiming that, after an odd look from a stranger, they had become impotent.

Only when the police, eyes presumably averted, dragged a suspect stranger to the police station was the mystery solved. He was not, he said, the actual evil eye but he did happen to have a cure for impotence, if required.

On investigation, it was discovered that he was part

of a team of car salesmen from Nigeria who had stage-managed the scare to boost sales in a magic potion for curing impotence.

UNKINDEST CHRISTENING PRESENT

A sixteen year-old girl had never met the boy who pushed her into a house and tried unsuccessfully to rape her but she did remember his name.

Everard Dick.

MOST CONFUSED PORNO STAR

Linda Lovelace was, for a brief period during the 1970s, a symbol of the new permissiveness. Her film *Deep Throat* made her internationally famous. She was interviewed by sex magazines. She appeared on chat shows. Her bestselling book started with the words, 'I live for sex, will never get enough of it.'

The true story of Linda Boreman was revealed in 1980 when she wrote *Ordeal* – the earlier books were apparently fakes. She tells the story of a small-town girl who was exploited, raped and brutalized by J. R. 'Chuck' Traynor, a Svengali figure who was her manager, pimp and husband. Far from living for sex, Linda hated it while she was with Chuck and claims she never had an orgasm during the six years they were together.

Utterly naive, she was trapped and bullied into a bewildering number of tacky sexual scenes including, quite early on in the relationship, a group scene with five men.

Linda was an unworldly girl at that time, as can be judged from her reaction when one of the men said, 'Let's make a sandwich'.

What an extraordinary time to be thinking about food, she thought.

MOST POINTLESS INVENTION

In Japan, now a plastic surgeon's paradise, a new invention is on the market: a plastic facsimile hymen to be fitted for the bride's wedding night.

MOST TYPICALLY AUSTRALIAN BIRDS

Naturalists in Australia have come up with a last-ditch attempt to encourage flamingoes to mate more often. They have put up mirrors in strategic places around the lake where they live.

The hope is that the few males left will look in the mirrors, believe there's some sexual competition from other males, and get to work immediately.

LEAST SURPRISING HEADLINE

NEWLY-WEDS, AGED 82, HAVE PROBLEM

Streatham News

TOP THREE CONTEMPORARY HANG-UPS

In a survey among men and women in their mid-twenties, sociologist Michael Schofield has discovered that 56 per cent of men and 59 per cent of women suffer from some sexual worry.

For the women, the top three hang-ups were:

1. Getting bored of sex.
2. Feeling guilty about it.
3. Doing it badly.

For men, the worries are:

1. Guilt (suffered by one in four men).
2. Doing it badly.
3. The effects of masturbation.

MOST RIGOROUS KEEPER OF
THE SABBATH

Making love on a Sunday was strictly forbidden by the Church until the late nineteenth century.

A methodist living in St Martin's Lane took this

19

edict further than most. He would tie the legs of his cockerel up on a Saturday night so that the henhouse was free of sin on the Sunday.

MOST MERCENARY GROPER

When accused of stealing £250 from a bank where she worked, Vlandine Tousel of Alençon placed the blame fairly and squarely on her new boyfriend Ermis, whom she had known some fifteen minutes. Vlandine explained what happened.

'I know men like big ones, so I filled up my brassière with notes. Ermis was fondling me behind the bank when he suddenly remembered an important engagement. I never saw him again.'

MOST VIRGINAL UNDERGRADUATES

A 1983 survey by the Oxford University magazine *Isis* suggested that Britain's most woefully inexperienced students are at Oxford – over 50 per cent of the undergraduates were virgins.

The most rampant university is Cardiff. There 77 per cent of students claimed to be enjoying regular sex.

LEAST ENJOYABLE IMPREGNATION

A bullet fired on 12 May 1865 during the American Civil War set in train an unusual course of events, according to the *Lancet* in 1875.

It first penetrated the left testicle of one of Grant's soldiers and then entered the side of a young woman who was ministering to the sick.

278 days later, the girl, who claimed she was a virgin, gave birth to an eight-pound boy. Her doctor, a Dr L. G. Capers of Vicksburg, Missouri, confirmed that she was still *virgo intacta*.

Three weeks later, he was called to see the baby, who had a pronounced swelling in the scrotum. The doctor operated and removed a battered piece of shot. At that moment, he concluded that the bullet had carried the sperm from the soldier to the girl, who had then been impregnated.

He found out where the soldier was and told him the story.

Later the couple were introduced to one another. They ended up marrying and produced three more children by the more direct method.

LEAST CONVINCING THEORY ABOUT MICK JAGGER

In her taboo-shattering recent book *The New Celibacy*, Dr Gabrielle Brown reveals a new aspect of Mick Jagger's character.

Mick, she says, is a practising celibate 'because it avoids a lot of problems'.

And what else can a poor boy do?

FREAKIEST CHILDHOOD EXPERIENCE

Counter-culture guru and author of *Bomb Culture*, Jeff
Nuttall has written of his first sexual stirrings and the
feelings of guilt and fear they aroused – even to the
extent of shaping his political attitudes.

Jeff was four and used to rub himself up against a
little girl of his own age. When two older boys found
out about this, they began to persecute him.

'They took me solemnly to the orchard where a rusty
pair of shears hung in a tree. They told me that without
any shadow of doubt if I ever fucked anyone again the
shears would be used on me. They told me that the full
power of the law and the knacker's yard hung over
me, that the copper had been round on his bike asking
that very afternoon.'

Later the boys subjected Jeff to mild sexual humili-
ations. The incident stayed with him throughout his
childhood, 'the worm in my rose'.

'From then,' he was to write years later, 'I learned
that the police are after my knackers.'

MOST IRISH SEX ADVICE

A helpful guide to young marrieds has been included
in a recent edition of the *Irish Sunday Press*. Part of it
reads:

'These refer to four separate stages in the consum-
mation of a marriage. (No marriage is valid in canon
law until it is consummated.) If any one of *erectio*,
introductio, *penetratio* or *ejeculatio* is absent – or if they

happen in the wrong order – the marriage is not properly consummated and thus not valid.'

STUPIDEST VIENNESE ARTIST

Johann Heer of Vienna was having an affair with Frau Gambul, the wife of a friend. In a post-coital moment, Frau Gambul switched on the television in the bedroom to watch *Gone With the Wind* and, as she lay there, Johann, an amateur artist, picked up a felt tip pen and drew a romantic landscape on her bum. Then he fell asleep. When he awoke, his lover had gone home to her husband.

Frau Gambul got into bed at home just before her husband, a taxi driver, returned home from his late shift. As he gave her a goodnight kiss, he noticed Johann Heer's landscape.

It was only when the couple compared the signature on Frau Gambul's bum to the one on a picture in the dining room that Johann had given them that she admitted what had happened.

The husband was granted a divorce.

MOST UNUSUAL UNDERARM DEODORANT

Among country folk in Maryland, young men once had to endure a particularly rigorous test before they were allowed to marry.

When a father noticed that his son was falling in love with a girl, he would acquire some of her excrement and make his son carry it around with him under his left armpit for several days.

If his enthusiasm for the girl was undiminished after this ordeal, the father would agree to the marriage.

NOSIEST CLERGYMAN

Father Bill McConalogue of the Church of St Mary and Joseph in East London believed that no young couple should enter the state of matrimony lightheartedly. So when Peter Lewis and Mandy Robinson asked him to marry them, he handed them a questionnaire 'to ensure', as the holy father put it, 'that they were adequately prepared.'

Among the questions were:

'How many times do you want to have intercourse on your wedding night?

Do you pick your nose?

Do you put the toilet seat down after using it?

Do you leave your toenail clippings lying about?

Do you pass gas often?

Do you burp?'

Peter and Mandy finally decided to get married in another church.

TWO

WITH MY BODY . . .

'Get off. You've done it . . . And your language is most revolting.'

His wife, as reported by Walter, author of My Secret Life *(1889)*

FLEET STREET'S WILDEST
BRIDEGROOM

A well-known Fleet Street editor had an unusual experience on his wedding night.

He was making love to his bride when his foot got caught in the bars of the electric fire. As the man yelped and writhed in agony, his new wife clung on to him passionately, convinced that he was in throes of ecstasy at her sexual expertise.

It was only when he started hopping around the bedroom with a smouldering foot that the truth dawned on her.

MOST MOVING FIRST NIGHT

Probably the most celebrated orgiast in history, Cesare Borgia had a particularly active wedding night. One of his guests substituted laxatives for some pills Borgia had ordered from the apothecary and he spent most of the night on the lavatory.

LEAST APPRECIATED
TELEVISION SHOW

A fifty-four-year-old spinster living in a block of flats in Nice called the police in when, night after night, her neighbours Claude and Josette Mercadier appeared on the flat's closed television circuit, making love.

Suspecting a case of exhibitionism *à deux*, the police inspector put the charges to Claude and Josette.

They were mortified. A few days ago they had, in a spirit of marital playfulness, decided to record their performances on video. What they didn't know was that a technical hitch by Claude was giving everyone in the block a free live show.

They were charged with indecency.

DOTTIEST OLD NAZI

Something went out of the life of a German ex-officer when he left the army shortly after the end of the war. He found that, out of uniform, he was almost impotent.

Luckily he could still make love to his wife – under the right conditions. First of all, he would hoist the German national flag over his house.

Then he would pin to his pyjama jacket the Iron Cross, the Close Combat Cross, The Panzer Storm Medal and two other lesser decorations. Finally he would put on his treasured stormtrooper helmet. Only then was he ready for his wife.

Unfortunately his problem didn't end there. His skin appeared to be allergic to the metal from his decorations and he tended to break out in a rather nasty rash.

31

CORRECTEST COMMUNIST ATTITUDES

Excessive sexual appetites and correct ideological attitudes do not go together, according to the official Chinese publication on the subject, *Information on Sex*.

The manual explains that no one is allowed to make love before the age of twenty-five and intercourse before marriage is regarded as a criminal activity. After marriage, couples are strongly advised against indulging themselves too often.

'If, on the morning after having sex, a couple feel worn out, heavy-headed, pain in the thighs or short of breath, or if they detect a loss of appetite, they are having too much and should take corrective measures'.

As for masturbation, which causes 'nervous weakness', the manual advises 'correct communist attitudes' and baggy underwear.

MOST RAMPANT PENSIONER

Marriage for shy, retiring, sexually inexperienced Rosalita was not at all what she expected.

Her new husband Giovanni Bomba, a widower of some seven years seemed so kind and gentle. When Giovanni and Rosalita became man and wife, he was seventy-six and she was seventy-five.

But during their honeymoon, Rosalita discovered the sort of man she had married. He was insatiable, demanding sex with her morning, noon and night.

When they returned to set up home in Rome, he would go out to buy porn magazines and ask her to imitate the wilder poses of the nude models.

At last Rosalita told Giovanni that this had to stop

– the pace was killing her. Infuriated, her husband hurled himself at her and attempted to murder her.

In court, Giovanni revealed that he had been advertising for a wife for some time before he met Rosalita but, he said, 'none of the women were good enough for me'.

LEAST ROMANTIC FIRST MORNING

In his book *Life After Marriage*, Al Alvarez gives a not entirely unbiased account of his first marriage.

He had known his bride for seven weeks before they got married and their first night was a major erotic failure. But, Al says, the worst surprise awaited him in the morning when he brought his new bride breakfast in bed after cleaning up downstairs.

The new Mrs Alvarez bit into her toast and then put it down in dismay.

'The crusts,' she said. 'You didn't cut off the crusts.'

With that, a marriage died but a book was born.

MOST DONG-FIXATED WIFE

Weddings and funerals were events of special significance for a local government official in Cologne. As soon as he heard the bells ringing, he would leave his office and hurry home to make love to his wife.

A divorce court in Cologne heard that the man's life

had become a misery after his wife had decided she could only make love while church bells rang. Since tape-recordings failed to do the trick, he had to wait until Sunday mornings – and those special events.

The court granted him a divorce.

LEAST CONVINCING SIGN OF INCREASING CIVILIZATION

The sale of wives by their husband, a common practice in the eighteenth and early nineteenth century, continued in some parts of England until around 1890.

Usually the wife was led into the market-place by her husband with a rope around her neck, paraded around the square, and then sold to the highest bidder.

Quite often, prices were extremely reasonable. In 1817, a wife was sold in Nottingham for threepence and, in 1884, one went for one penny (with a dinner thrown in).

The sale of wives at these so-called 'ham markets' was regarded as a perfectly acceptable form of commerce. *The Times* of 22 July 1797 reported:

'By an oversight in the report on Smithfield Market we are not in a position to quote this week the price of women. The increasing value of the fairer sex is considered by various celebrated writers to be a sure sign of increasing civilization. On the ground Smithfield may raise a claim to rank as a place of special advance in refinement, for at its Market the price of women has lately risen from half a guinea to three guineas and a half.'

CRUELLEST QUALIFYING ROUND
FOR INTERNATIONAL MASTERMIND

When the wife of Erwin Gehlen first refused to make love until he had answered three riddles correctly, it seemed no more than one of married life's little games, he told a court in Stockholm.

'But then,' said Erwin, 'the riddles got harder as the years passed. It finally reached the stage when I was lucky to solve three a year.'

GREATEST ACT OF
MARITAL FIDELITY

In 1937, the *Daily Mail* reported an extreme case of wifely devotion. The young and beautiful wife of a Genoese businessman was admired so much by men who saw her that the husband became insanely jealous.

So she took steps to remedy the matter and disfigured her face by pouring acid over it.

'I could not prevent men from admiring my beauty,' she said, 'but in future they will not look at me and I shall be happy.'

MOST TEDIOUSLY PURE WIFE

The view that decent women should have no sexual feelings, quite popular in middle class society in Victorian times, was propounded with most authority by the eminent venerologist William Acton.

He quotes a particular case-history:

'She assured me that she felt no sexual passions whatever; that if she was capable of them, they were dormant. Her passion for her husband was a Platonic kind, and far from wishing to stimulate his frigid feelings, she doubted whether it would be right or not ... I believe this lady is a perfect ideal of an English wife and mother, kind, considerate, self-sacrificing, and sensible, so pure-hearted as to be utterly ignorant of and averse to any sensual indulgence.'

Historians have speculated as to whether this paragon might not have been Mrs Acton.

MOST VOLATILE
NEWLY-MARRIED COUPLE

The honeymoon of Istvan and Marcia Havas started badly. Soon after Istvan had carried Marcia over the threshold of their new flat, he remarked that he did not like the green curtains. A furious row ensued, during which Istvan stormed out of the flat.

As he reached the street below, he was stopped in his tracks by his new wife who, in a state of high emotion, was climbing out of their window on the second floor. She jumped, and he tried to catch her.

When the couple were taken to hospital, it was discovered that Istvan had a broken leg, and Marcia a broken neck.

LOUDEST PROOF THAT THE FAMILY THAT PLAYS TOGETHER STAYS TOGETHER

Ksar Hellal of Tunisia became famous overnight when President Bourguiba revealed the dimensions of his musical family in a broadcast appeal for better family planning.

'He is the father of forty children, born to him by four wives, with whom he had created a complete orchestra,' said the president. 'This is something which is utterly scandalous.'

MUMMY'S DIRTIEST TRICK

In an unusual case, a twenty-eight-year-old man divorced his wife on the grounds of five words which she used to say at crucial intimate moments.

It first happened two months after the wedding and then became a habit.

'When Gerda said those words,' the husband told the court, 'I could no longer make love. I begged her never to use the silly phrase again. I pleaded with her.'

37

But nothing worked and he became a total failure in bed.

The words were: 'Give it all to mummy.'

SADDEST MODERN PARABLE

When the bridegroom of a young Arab girl discovered on their wedding night that she was not a virgin, he immediately told his father, who in turn spoke to the girl's father and uncle. Between them decided that she should die.

In fact, dying was not bad enough for her. The family should murder her four times: by throwing her from a mountain, stabbing her with a knife, drowning her in a well and drowning her again in a local lake.

For some reason or other, this elaborate plan was abandoned in favour of a more prosaic approach. A few days later, the bride's father and uncle grabbed the girl while the rest of the neighbourhood were at another wedding, and poured pesticide down her throat, poisoning her.

There is some piquancy in the setting of this crime. It all came to pass in 1977 in Nazareth.

MOST OFTEN INTERRUPTED
HONEYMOON COUPLE

It was some time before honeymoon couple Mr and Mrs Arthur Millbank noticed that the mattress on which they were making love had caught fire.

Then Mr Millbank leapt up, humped the smouldering mattress downstairs and left it in a corner.

The couple were just picking up where they left off – now on the bare springs of the bed – when firemen, called in by the neighbours whose fence was now on fire, burst into the room.

LEAST BALANCED ACCOUNT OF
WEDDED BLISS

To judge from *Against Marriage* an anonymous pamphlet published in 1690 and later ascribed to the Earl of Rochester, marriage at that time was far from being a garden of delights:

Husband, thou dull unpitied miscreant,
Wedded to Noise, to Misery, and Want;
Sold an Eternal Vassall for thy Life,
Oblig'd to Cherish and to Heat a Wife . . .
Marry'd! O Hell and Furies! Name it not,
Hence, hence you Holy Cheats; a Plot, a Plot!
By day 'tis nothing but an endless Noise;
By night the Echo of Forgotten Joys.

39

THREE

HOMEBREAKERS

'The prerequisite for a good
marriage . . . is the license to be
unfaithful.'

Carl Jung

COLDEST YAYA

Yaya Rahim, the local handyman in an Iranian village, had two problems. One was that he couldn't resist seducing other men's wives and the other was that he had bright ginger hair and a crooked nose, unusual characteristics in those parts.

After no less than six wives had given birth to babies with bright ginger hair and a crooked nose, the men of the village took action. On a freezing night they took him to the top of a mountain and left him there – without any trousers.

Yaya's extremities suffered badly from frostbite and doctors say he may never make love again.

MOST THOROUGH CAVITY SEARCH

Frankfurt dentist Dr Richard Sternernagel specialized in society women – and did not limit his investigations to their teeth.

Above his surgery was what the press was later to call 'a luxurious love-nest'. There were mirrors everywhere, a four poster bed, black sheets and other non-dental equipment. There the forty-six-year-old dentist had seduced three hundred women.

Elke Gerlach was his last. Twenty-two-year-old Elke was Nicholas Gerlach's second wife, his first marriage having ended in divorce after Inge, the first Mrs Gerlach was lured into Sternernagel's famous room.

A friend of the dentist, Gerlach begged him to stay clear of his new wife. But Elke needed to have a tooth filled one day.

When Gerlach called to collect his wife, he found the

surgery locked. Racing upstairs, he discovered the couple in an active love-nest situation. He pulled out a pistol and fired six bullets into the dentist.

'He promised not to destroy my happiness,' he was later to tell the jury at his trial for murder.

MOST BOXED IN EX-HUSBAND

Alex Wartley took it very badly when his wife ran off with a chimney-sweep. He vowed he would never have anything to do with women again and, just to make sure, he lived for the rest of his life in a green wooden box five feet long, four foot high and three foot deep, which he kept in the garden of Mr David Moreau.

After his death at the age of eighty, Alex's feat was submitted to the Guinness Book of Records. He had lived thirty-five years in the box.

WORST ORGANIZED CRIME OF PASSION

When a petrol bomb was thrown through a bedroom window in Florida, police assumed it must be a crime of passion. Inside, a married woman was in bed with her lover.

At last a clue was discovered. The bottle that was thrown had originally contained prune juice and it

was known that the woman's husband suffered from serious constipation.

Hardly surprising, since he was 78.

MOST DEMANDING HEAD OF THE HOUSEHOLD

The trial of Mervyn, Lord Castlehaven, in 1631 was somewhat unusual. His lordship was tried for 'Abetting a Rape upon his Countess, Committing Sodomy with his servants, and Commanding and Countenancing the Debauching of his daughter.'

One after another, the witnesses provided an insight into the Castlehavens' home life.

His wife Lady Audley revealed that 'the first or second night after we were married, Antill (a servant) came to our bed ... He made Skipwith (another servant) come naked into our Chamber and bed: and took delight in calling his servants to show their nudities, and forced me to look upon them and to commend those that had the longest.'

Her ladyship then explained how another servant was encouraged to rape her, while her husband 'held my hands and one of my feet ... He delighted to see the Act done.'

Lord Glenhaven's daughter added to the story. 'I was first persuaded to lie with Skipwith by the Earl's persuasion and threatenings ... He saw Skipwith and I lie together several times and so did many Servants of the house besides ... He used Oyl to enter my body first, for I was then but twelve years of age.'

To complete the picture, a number of servants gave evidence. One said that, after he had raped Lady

Castlehaven, the earl 'used my body as a woman', while another testified that most of the servants had been to bed with him.

Unsatisfied by all this, Glenhaven had employed a woman called Blandina 'a Common Whore to his Lordship and his servants'. She was once abused by the head of the house and his servants/lovers 'for the space of seven hours, until she got the French Pox'.

Castlehaven's defence – that his servants had been invited into his bed because of a temporary lack of space in the house – was rejected by the jury and he was sentenced to death.

STUPIDEST ADULTERER

When Anna married Esteban in Mexico City, she discovered that he suffered from a harmless, if bizarre, peculiarity. He could only make love to the sound of rousing march music.

For a couple of years, all was well between Anna and Esteban, so long as his gramophone and marching tunes were in the bedroom, ready for use when required.

But when Esteban insisted on taking the gramophone with him on business trips, his wife became suspicious.

She hired a private detective and followed him to a hotel. They waited outside the door until a deafening march announced that Esteban was on the job.

Bursting into the room, they found the music-lover making vigorous love to his mistress.

HEAVIEST PENALTY FOR
COITUS INTERRUPTUS

That famous Biblical character Onan's solution to what would now be called a 'no-win situation', and its unfortunate result, is recorded in Genesis:

'And Judah said unto Onan, Go unto thy brother's wife, and marry her, and raise up seed to thy brother. And Onan knew that the seed should not be his: and it came to pass, when he went in unto his brother's wife, that he spilled it on the ground, lest that he should give seed to his brother. And the thing which he did did displease the Lord; and wherefore He slew him also.'

CURIOUSEST CUCKOLD

An eighteenth-century nobleman who discovered his wife in bed with an officer took his revenge in a somewhat eccentric way.

He tied them both naked to the bedposts and left them there without food or water for four days.

His friends and neighbours were invited in to enjoy the spectacle.

MOST DISASTROUS WIFE SWOP

It took the police some time to work out the background to a bloody pitched battle that took place one Sunday afternoon between two neighbouring families in Devizes, Wiltshire.

It all began innocently enough when Malcolm and Theresa Taylor and their neighbours Clive and Annette Barford decided to swop partners. But then one day Malcolm and his new bed-mate Annette decided they preferred the original arrangement. Next door, Clive Barford and Theresa weren't so sure – they rather liked it like this.

Tempers became frayed when Malcolm's stepfather Frederick Edwards (who to confuse the police still further lived with his stepson) was involved in a discussion with Clive Barford about the situation which got out of hand. Within the next few minutes, an unneighbourly fracas had broken out, during which:

1. Clive was hit in the face by Fred.
2. Clive threw a glass through Malcolm's window.
3. Theresa Taylor came out to join in, wielding a kitchen knife.
4. Malcolm hit his wife on the head with a branch.
5. Fred also hit Theresa, but he used a pickaxe handle.
6. Clive knocked Fred to the ground and started kicking his head in.
7. All five were later taken to hospital for treatment.

MOST STARTLED SEX KITTEN

Mrs Elvira Babsezian of Struttgart was bored with her particularly inactive husband, so she placed an anonymous advertisement in the local paper, saying 'SEX KITTEN SEEKS SHARP CAT'.

Elvira received several replies, including one from her husband which contained a nude photograph of himself.

'It is the first time I have seen him naked in fourteen years of marriage,' she said.

MOST NEGATIVE CALIFORNIAN

A couple in California had only been married three weeks when the wife discovered that her new husband was already married. She threw him out of the house.

Before he left, the man locked his wife up in a chastity belt made out of nylon and a triple-padlocked chain, which he had specially constructed for her.

The police had to be called in to release her.

MOST DISLOYAL HUSBAND

The Director of the Marriage Council of Philadelphia, Dr Harold Lief, tells his patients the true story of a man, released by a New York hospital after a serious illness.

'Don't get too excited about sex for a while,' his doctor told him.

'Okay,' the man said, 'I'll just make love to my wife.'

WORST ORGANIZED SPECTATOR SPORT

In the GP's journal *Medical Interface*, a doctor reported a particularly baffling case. Two of his patients, a married couple of thirty and twenty-eight, came to his surgery to ask his help in sorting out their marriage, which was in severe difficulty. They also brought the man's eighteen-year-old mistress.

The problem, they said, was simple.

The man enjoyed making love to his mistress, but only when watched by his wife. The wife also enjoyed watching but was less interested when her husband asked to watch her with other men.

Eventually she did manage to sleep with another man but not quite as her loving husband had planned – she chose his best friend for a secret affair.

Unfortunately the husband stumbled in on the un-scheduled floor show.

He was, said the doctor, upset and wounded by the whole business.

NASTIEST CASE OF
MARITAL NEEDLE

A thirty-year-old man who found his wife in bed with the milkman, refused to believe her story that he was helping her mend the bedside lamp.

He decided to ensure his wife's fidelity while he was away at work, teaching in a nearby town, by sewing her up with a needle and thread.

'He forced her to sit on a chair in the nude,' reported a police officer, 'while he performed the delicate and very painful chastity surgery on Monday mornings before leaving her. He took threads out on Friday evenings when he came home to spend the weekends with her.'

It was five weeks before the pain became too much to bear. The wife went to see a doctor, who called in the police.

UNLUCKIEST ATHENIAN ADULTERER

There are 70,000 taxis in Athens but, a Greek court heard, the co-respondent in the case chose the wrong one.

Having taken a taxi to his married lover's address and let himself in with his key, he was surprised to find a few minutes later that the taxi-driver had a key, too.

It was his house.

MOST CONSCIENTIOUS
MOTHER-IN-LAW

Zuleka Kacane of Albania wanted nothing but the best for her eighteen-year-old daughter Marya. So when Marya announced that she wanted to marry a young man called Enver, Zuleka insisted that he should pass a test before she would consent.

When Enver arrived at the house for his test, Zuleka greeted him at the door in a skimpy nightie. Then she took him to her bedroom and bolted the door.

As the test started in earnest, twenty women, led by Enver's mother, burst into the room and beat Zuleka up.

A tearful Marya later commented, 'I begged mother not to insist on the test. I knew he would pass it.'

BEST MALE ARGUMENT FOR
THE MISSIONARY POSITION

Anna May Reese's husband worked out an elaborate, if somewhat extreme, method of repaying her infidelity – he would blow her up as she made love to her boyfriend.

Having put a stick of dynamite between the mattress and the bed, he ran a fuse under the floorboards to a spot outside the house. With his ear to the wall, he heard the couple making love and lit the fuse.

Anna May was killed. Her boyfriend suffered slightly burnt hands.

FOUR

PROBLEM PAGES

'Can you set our minds at rest? Please tell me if kissing my wife's breasts can cause cancer.'

Letter to the Sunday People, 1983

WETTEST LOVER

The strange case of a man who could only make love when his feet were submerged in cold water has been reported by sex therapist Dr Robert Chartham.

The man would run the cold tap and sit on the edge of the bath with his feet submerged. His long-suffering wife would then lower herself on to his lap.

The situation began to get out of hand when the wife found that, as soon as the cold tap turned off, she turned off too.

Eventually Dr Chartham came up with a solution – a plastic bag full of ice cubes down the bed – which got the couple out of the bathroom and satisfactorily back in the bedroom.

'I suspected the patient acted in this way because he had his first sexual experience while wading in the sea,' the triumphant doctor reported. 'But it was not so.'

MOST UNGRATEFUL BRIDEGROOM

Reporting to the Royal Society of Medicine a doctor revealed an unusual case of sexual insecurity.

One of his patients, a brilliant honours student was pressed into an early marriage with his girlfriend by her parents, who provided him with money and a flat.

But all was not well with the young couple. Despite having a satisfactory sex life while unmarried, the bridegroom's sense that he was now a kept man rendered him completely impotent.

Only when he obtained his degree, a job, a salary and his self-esteem could normal service be resumed.

SADDEST STORY FROM CLUBLAND

The 10th Duke of Marlborough was, according to the gossips at his club White's, finding the strain of his recent marriage to Laura, the new duchess, rather a strain.

When a member asked him if he was finding it all too arduous, the Duke shook his head sadly.

'Mr Mouse won't come out to play any more,' he said.

SILLIEST OLD SCOTSMAN

According to Mr Leonard Cracker, a pensioner from Aberdeen, a 'mob' of loving couples would habitually make 'loud and disgusting noises' in a lovers' lane near his house. Infuriated, he grabbed his knobkerrie, a souvenir from the First World War, went out into the lane and belaboured the first couple he found, inflicting wounds that later required six stitches apiece.

Mr and Mrs Donald Worse were taken aback by the incident since they were not a courting twosome but a married couple of some twenty years.

'We called in for a kiss and a cuddle,' said Mrs Worse. 'Suddenly we were overwhelmed by a madman.'

A court was told that it was Mr Cracker's fourteenth offence of this kind.

MOST DISASTROUS CALIFORNIAN ORGASM

The briefest, most explosive and dramatic sex life in the world is that experienced by the clams who live, appropriately enough, on the west coast of America.

Once a year, the adult clams emerge from the mud to mate. Each female, now full of eggs, is followed by several males. As the sperm cells are released from the male, two things happen: his body bursts and he sinks dying back into the mud. The stimulus releases the eggs from the female's body which also bursts and dies.

WHAT'S NOT UP, DOC?

The world famous author of *Baby and Child Care*, Dr Benjamin Spock, had an unpromising introduction to sex. After what he called a Victorian upbringing, he was so traumatized by events surrounding his loss of virginity, that for years he was impotent. Finally, psychiatric help did the trick.

LEAST SUCCESSFUL BLOW JOB

A medical journal has recorded a case of coital foreplay that went tragically wrong.

In a moment of *tendresse*, a man had the impulse to

blow into his lover's vagina. This he did vigorously, not knowing that, since she had just stopped menstruating, her vascular system was directly vulnerable.

She complained of pains immediately and was dead within a few minutes.

MOST WORRYING SEX SURVEY

Sexually speaking, India is going through a serious recession at present, according to Dr A. G. Nadu of the All Indian Institute of Technology.

'Many soldiers cut short their annual leave because of sexual frustrations in civilian life,' says the doctor, 'and businessmen and extremely rich people are not keen on sex under any circumstances.'

ODDEST COUPLE

The sex life of a 6′ 4″ policeman and his wife became too complicated for them and they ended up consulting a local doctor.

The wife said she could only make love to her burly husband when he was dressed in a frilly pink negligée.

This all went well until the policeman had a request. If *he* wore the negligée, would *she* wear a gas-mask?

They both decided they needed help.

MOST FLAWED SEXUAL DIET

It was an unusual diet, but quite an effective one. When a Cambridgeshire farmer's wife decided to lose weight by instituting a strict regime of particularly arduous sexual practices, she reduced her weight from twenty-one stone to sixteen in a matter of months.

The only snag was that the course had, by its nature, to be taken by the woman's husband, a slim six-footer. Its effect on him was so shattering that one day he blacked out while driving his tractor.

When he went to see the doctor, he was found to weigh five stone.

WORST NEWS FOR FLAT-CHESTED AIR STEWARDESSES

The US Medical Association have warned air stewardesses that it is unwise to have silicone implants to improve breast measurements.

They are liable to explode at high altitudes.

MOST INSECURE NOVELIST

'I know wimmins and wimmins is difficult,' Ernest Hemingway once told a friend, and his own life bears out the comment.

Married four times, Hemingway talked and wrote

about sex rather more than he enjoyed it. His joyless womanizing and hatred of homosexuality – on one occasion in Madrid he smashed an obvious homosexual in the face just for the hell of it – have suggested to some that he was insecure about his masculinity.

His friend Sidney Franklin revealed that Hemingway's great worry was about the size of his penis.

' 'Bout the size of a thirty-thirty shell,' said Franklin.

SECOND MOST INSECURE NOVELIST

The sex life of F. Scott Fitzgerald was, despite his much-publicized affair with Zelda, marked by a pronounced lack of self-confidence.

Fitzgerald was particularly worried that he failed to 'measure up' to other men. He consulted his friend Ernest Hemingway with whom he compared members, finding them about the same size (not, in view of Hemingway's own hang-ups, that this was too reassuring). Since his friend was still unconvinced, Hemingway took him to the Louvre to look at the statues. Even that failed to restore Fitzgerald's self-esteem.

His last mistress Sheilah Graham touched glancingly on the subject in her autobiography, although her defence of Fitzgerald's dimensions would not have reassured him.

'Personally,' she wrote, 'given the choice between a donkey and a chipmunk, I might choose the latter.'

COITUS MOST INTERRUPTUS

A naked young couple making love on a river bank near Bedford disturbed various members of the public who were boating on the river, and complaints were made to the police.

A woman police constable was despatched to the scene of the crime but, when she asked them to move along, they ignored her – even when she grabbed the man's arm and tried to disengage him.

After several minutes' unsuccessful pleading, a panda car was summoned and the police team managed to separate, dress and place under arrest the rampant couple.

An hour after they had been charged and released from the police station, they were at it again – in the same place. Another policewoman found them and asked them to stop it at once.

'Oh no,' came the anguished reply. 'Not again! Give us a break, will you?'

But she didn't. The couple were fined £20 for breaking two by-laws.

MOST SELF-DISCIPLINED
POLICEMAN

Appearing for the defence in an immoral earnings case, Detective Derek Pollard told a court that he had, in the line of duty, visited the seaside massage parlour of Mrs Pamela Brown.

Mrs Brown, described in newspaper reports as 'a statuesque blonde' asked the detective to take off all his clothes and then rubbed baby lotion into his body.

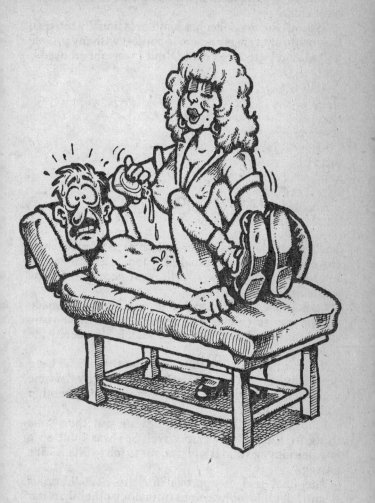

'You're a Johnston's baby now,' she is reported to have said.

'During the massage, her hand occasionally brushed the inside of my legs and made contact with my private parts,' said Detective Pollard, 'but I was not aroused.'

MOST SERIOUS CASES OF SEXUAL BOREDOM

The sex problem most openly discussed in magazines since 1981 has been sexual boredom – a total lack of interest in physical love, or 'sexual anorexia' as one journalist put it.

Luckily the new generation of rock stars have made sexlessness as chic as promiscuity was fifteen years ago. Johnny Rotten of the Sex Pistols pioneered the new maturity.

'I don't hate sex,' he said, 'it's just that it's all been done between the ages of twelve and now. By the time you're twenty, you just think – yawn – just another squelch session.'

Phil Oakey of the Human League put the whole thing in a historical perspective: 'Sex was built up a few decades ago and it's just about to fall to bits . . . It's boring.'

The final seal of approval for the new 'Limp is Beautiful' philosophy comes from none other than star and folk hero Boy George.

'It's funny,' he says, 'I don't miss having a sex life . . . I'd rather have a cup of tea and a good conversation.'

MOST DISASTROUS STAND-UP ACT

Comedian Sid Deakes has an unfortunate source of new material for his act. What he calls his 'precious part' has disappeared.

'I have a girlfriend,' said sixty-five-year-old Sid, 'but a serious relationship is out of the question . . . It has vanished.'

Sid believes that his problem dates back to a series of operations he had several years ago and is seeking compensation. Meanwhile he will continue to work the clubs.

'So far the audience don't know about my loss,' Sid told the *Daily Mirror*. 'I'll make a joke about it. I haven't thought of one yet but something will come up, I hope.'

LEAST IMPRESSIVE SEXUAL HANG-UP

In 1977 the hippy magazine *OZ* included this letter in its agony column:

'Whenever my boyfriend and I have intercourse, during each stroke his balls slap against my body.

'In addition to this being painful for him, the slapping sound is so amusing that we have to momentarily stop because we start laughing.

'We have thought of taping his balls to his torso. Is there any other solution to our problem?'

The letter was signed 'Slap Happy'.

FIVE

STRANGELY BRITISH

'Oh, Sir James, can I have no more fun
in bed?'

Queen Victoria to her doctor

LEAST SUCCESSFUL FLOOR SHOW

There was an unusual attraction in the back room of
the Crown Hotel, near Southampton. Every Sunday
lunch Mrs Paula Novak would spread chocolate drops
all over her body and invite men in the audience to eat
them off her. As part of her act, a court was told by PC
Bowers of the city's vice squad, men would remove
her black stockings while she put her foot in their
groin.

When interrupted by the defence who asked whether
'that would depend on whether he dressed to the left
or the right,' Bowers replied, 'No, I've always found a
man's genitals to be in the same area.'

However the shows were a flop, claimed Mr David
Elger QC.

'Mrs Novak went down like a lead balloon,' he said.

MOST FAMOUS EROTIC FAILURE
IN REGENTS PARK

It was a case that captured the nation's imagination.

Dr Brian Richards was called to an unusual emergency in Regents Park. A couple, overcome by passion,
had just discovered why it is unwise to try to make
love in the front of an Austin Healy Sprite sports car.

At the critical moment, the man slipped a disc,
trapping his girlfriend. Near naked, neither of them
could move an inch. Finally the girl managed to
summon help by jamming her foot on the car horn.
Soon the car was surrounded by firemen, ambulance-
men, a number of highly amused onlookers and Dr
Richards.

'When we opened the door,' said the doctor, 'the man's bare rump, trousers and his ankles, lay as if transfixed on the near nude female torso. Two women volunteers had appeared to serve hot sweet tea in the best blitz style.'

Finally, firemen had to cut away the car's back panel, rear window and boot. The man was taken away in the ambulance and, as the girl was helped into a dressing-gown, she burst into floods of tears.

The doctor comforted her – her lover would soon be on the mend.

'Sod him,' she said. 'What's worrying me is how I'm going to explain to my husband what's happened to his car.'

NOISIEST LOVER

There are quiet and noisy lovers. Janet Huxley was one of the noisy ones.

Unfortunately for the neighbours she and her boy-friend had a particularly active sex life. One night, their neighbour Frank Sammes could bear it no longer. He burst into their flat, and pulled them apart shouting, 'Pack it in, I want to get some sleep.'

He then hit them both with a lamp.

When charged with assault, Sammes pleaded without success that he was acting with the best of motives.

'I thought someone was being beaten up or worse,' he said. 'I rushed upstairs to prevent a tragedy.'

MOST BRITISH ORGY

The editor of *Screw* magazine, Al Goldstein, found that his first orgy in Britain was more formal than he was used to.

'Soon as I arrived, I was told to take my clothes off and queue up for my food,' said Goldstein. 'The hostess insisted that we ate everything up before the orgy. I don't feel people were enjoying themselves much.'

LEAST RELIABLE WITNESS

Two girls from Prestwick claimed in a Scottish court they had been approached by a man who had offered them £1 each to 'jump on him, kick him and walk on him'.

When asked by the Procurator-Fiscal if they could see the man in court, one of the girls pointed to the court shorthand writer.

She was asked to think again.

MOST UNUSUAL COUNCIL DEMAND

Mr Ron Hawes, Housing Manager of Barking and Dagenham Council, gave council tenants some brisk advice when they complained of damp in their flat: cut down on your lovemaking and the damp will go.

According to Mr Hawes, every time Tina and Paul

Haswell made love, their heavy breathing increased condensation in the flat. Hence the dampness problem.

'Of course, we don't want Mr and Mrs Haswell to stop having normal relationships together,' said Mr Hawes, reasonably, 'but if they could help us, it would make the flat more hospitable.'

LEAST SUCCESSFUL WI EVENING

A local WI theatrical evening unfortunately had to be cancelled after it was found that every single member of the cast – seven women and a cat – had become pregnant.

The play was called *World Without Men*.

MOST SURPRISING CAUSE FOR NATIONAL PRIDE

A survey conducted by Dr Robert Chartham and quoted in G. L. Simon's *Book of World Sexual Records* will make the British male swell with pride.

The doctor took a sample of penis size by race and recorded the largest in each group. I will declare the result in reverse order:

France	7¾ inches
Sweden	7¾ inches
America	7¾ inches

Denmark	8 inches
West Germany	8½ inches
Great Britain	10½ inches

Well done, Carruthers!

UNHEALTHIEST VIBRATIONS

Staff at Crawley Hospital in Sussex were at a loss to explain how the hospital's television service had been out of action one evening.

The source of the problem was to be found in an isolation ward where a girl patient was illicitly entertaining her boyfriend in bed.

When asked how their behaviour could have affected television reception, he added coyly that the couple were using 'an electrical aid to love'.

LEAST SUCCESSFUL KNEE-TREMBLER

A Taunton man's revels at the Broomfield fair during the early seventeenth century ended rather more abruptly than he anticipated.

During the evening, rather drunk on cider, he found 'a willing wench' and went off to make love with her.

He pushed her up against what appeared to be a reasonably firm tree and suddenly all hell broke loose. The couple had chosen not a tree but the ceremonial pole erected for the festival and so enthusiastic were they that the bells at the top of the pole rang out across the village.

Soon the couple were no longer alone.

MOST EMOTIONAL CIVIC FUNCTIONARY

The Sheriff of Doncaster had had 'a long and tiring day of civic duties', but the final straw was when he was disturbed by a courting couple (aged 77 and 83) beneath his bedroom window.

He attacked them and was later fined £20 for assault.

BRAVEST DO-IT-YOURSELF CAMPAIGN

A Cheltenham man has launched an unusual campaign on behalf of what he calls 'DIY enthusiasts'.

In a letter to a sex magazine, he explains that he first became a DIY enthusiast at school. Later he met Jennifer who, being the daughter of a policeman, refused to make love to him. 'So,' he says, 'once more masturbation became the order of the day.'

The man is convinced that the time is ripe for a nationwide campaign.

'As a life-long wanker myself,' he writes, 'I feel that it is high time that wanking was brought right out of the closet in the same way that homosexuality has been.'

LEAST POPULAR ROVING MECHANIC

People in Blackhill, County Durham were astonished by the number of breakdowns that were taking place in the town. Luckily there was always somebody around to help out.

That somebody was Maurice Poulter. Maurice was particularly speedy at repairing broken down cars – hardly surprising, since it was Maurice who had sabotaged them in the first place.

'Doing this gives me some sort of sexual pleasure,' he told a court in Durham, explaining how he would watch out for girls who parked their cars in the town, disconnect a plug while they were shopping, and appear on the scene to help as they struggled unsuccessfully to start the engine.

Maurice was arrested after detectives saw him let down the front tyre of a twenty-five year old woman's mini and loosen a wire under its bonnet. When she returned, he offered to help but was arrested instead.

Appealing for leniency, Maurice said he had difficulty relating to women.

'I just can't seem to talk to them,' he said, 'I haven't had a woman for a long time.'

LEAST DESIRABLE ADDRESS

While London's Maiden Lane and Love Lane retain their ancient names, there is one street in Moorgate which the civic authorities saw fit to re-name in the fifteenth century.

It was called Gropecuntlane.

MOST ILL-JUDGED DECLARATION
OF LOVE

The traditional way for respectable people to make love is quietly and with decorum. Such appears to be the lesson to be learnt from the sad case of Colonel Valentine Baker, whose behaviour caused a major scandal during the 1870s.

Colonel Baker was a distinguished soldier and a friend of the Prince of Wales. One day he was travelling by train and found himself alone in a compartment with a pretty, coquettish girl called Miss Dickenson. They flirted and she made as if to sleep. The colonel moved in and began to caress her body; she, according to later reports, accepted and responded to his caresses. But then he made his big mistake. He uttered a sound.

'My darling, my ducky,' he said – and all hell broke loose.

Miss Dickerson, alarmed by these shameless words, leapt up and called for help. As a result, the colonel was tried, jailed and cashiered from his regiment in utter disgrace.

No less than ten years later, fellow officers presented a petition, requesting his reinstatement as an officer but the pride of Victorian womanhood rose as one to protest against such a move.

There were outraged letters to the press. 'His presence is an insult to every woman in the nation,' said one; another was astonished that a British officer could bring himself to shake hands with such a man; yet another claimed that the mere mention of his name in polite company was an act of gross indecency.

The petition failed and the colonel's shame was complete.

LEAST GRATEFUL PENFRIEND

A girl near Stoke-on-Trent received over 700 letters from a Formosan that she met on holiday.

Then she married the postman.

MOST FREQUENT PREMATURE EJACULATORS

Agony columnists have remarked that, of all the male sexual problems, premature ejaculation seems to be most widespread. Marie Stopes went further in her book *Enduring Passion*, which was published in 1928.

'The wide prevalence of premature ejaculation in British men of the professional and upper classes has surprised me. I have little evidence of its existence as a "problem" in the homes of manual workers, and incline to think it much rarer than among the "black-coated". Among Public School and University men it is one of the marital difficulties oftenest brought to my notice.'

UNKINDEST PRESS REPORT

In a despatch from London, the *Washington Post* reported:

'Last August, a man was found wandering in the grounds claiming he was in love with Princess Anne. He was found to be mentally disturbed.'

79

ODDEST EXCUSE FOR A STREET PARTY

There was only one thing unusual about a festival being held towards the end of the eighteenth century around the streets of the East End of London. Instead of a maypole, the procession was following a group of sailors who held aloft a ship's mast decked in streamers. Strapped to the mast were a naked man and woman.

The woman's husband, a ship's captain, had decided on this festive form of punishment when he discovered her in *flagrante delicto* with one of his sailors.

SIX

FOREIGN PARTS

'She had a gift. I was off on the nicest
dream of Berlin nightclubs . . . she
was giving a short lecture with her
tongue on the habits of the Germans,
the French, the English (one sorry bite
indeed), the Italians, the Spanish, she
must have had an Arab or two.'

Norman Mailer

MOST ORIGINAL DISH OF THE DAY

Because of the heat, a woman in West Africa was in the habit of keeping her contraceptive jelly in the fridge.

That is, until the day her cook served an unusual dish at a dinner party – a sherry trifle, decorated with cream, glace cherries, nuts and a delicate ring of pink gelatin pessaries.

MOST ELABORATE YUGOSLAVIAN JOKE

The staff of the Hotel Splendid on the Adriatic island of Korcula found the gross behaviour of the fifty German businessmen and their girlfriends, who had rented the hotel for a fortnight, too much to take.

One night, the head waiter Jorge Miroslav and two accomplices laced the party's champagne with a potent sleeping draught. Once unconscious, the guests were stripped naked, smothered in cherry jam and left in a sticky pile in the hotel lounge.

LEAST ATTRACTIVE EXHIBITIONIST

Otto Muehl's organization in Holland, the Sexual Egalitarian and Libertarian Fraternity was an earthier outfit than it sounds. Otto used to lead the Fraternity in various 'happenings'.

In Frankfurt, he cut off a goose's head, put a condom on it and subjected it to unusual last rites with his naked girlfriend. Chickens were similarly treated on other occasions.

But the Wet Dream Festival in Amsterdam was to be Otto's finest hour. He planned to explode a cow and invite spectators to participate in an orgy in its warm entrails.

Unfortunately, killjoy officials banned the zany Dutchman's madcap pranks.

SILLIEST CAMPAIGN

Until recently there was an organization in America entitled, somewhat inaccurately, The Society for Indecency to Naked Animals.

Worried by the naked sex organs on animals, the society's principal efforts were dedicated to designing garments to cover the offending parts of dogs, cows and horses.

MOST EVENTFUL WEDDING DAY

An astrologer in Surakarta, Indonesia, warned the parents of a young girl called Sakala that they should change the day of her wedding, but they went ahead anyway. Wrongly.

During the ceremony, Sakala fainted. While rushing

84

her to hospital, a friend was pulled in by the police for speeding. A bridesmaid, who was also in the car, got out to explain the situation but was hit by a bus and killed instantly.

Seeing the accident, Sakala suffered a massive heart attack and died minutes later in the arms of the bridegroom.

MOST DISASTROUS FAMILY
MISUNDERSTANDING

In love with his neighbour's daughter, Yugoslavian Mr Dorsan Yilmaz agreed to elope with her.

When the night arrived, he smuggled her down a ladder in a blanket and bundled her quickly into his car. After driving five miles, he took the blanket off — to reveal the girl's grandmother.

Then the enraged granny beat him up.

HARSHEST SEX LAW

In Cambodia, the Khmer Rouge regime has made the act of sex outside marriage a capital offence.

In this case, sex can include a casual remark made by a man to a woman — a mild flirtation has frequently led to the firing squad.

86

WORST CASE OF SATURDAY
NIGHT FEVER

Majorcan waiter Paco Vila seemed to have a lot going for him. He had really practised his dancing and, at the local disco, the foreign girls were there for the taking. Paco particularly liked the look of big-busted Scottish girls.

Unfortunately he was so skinny that no girl looked at him twice.

Then Paco hit on a solution – he would wear extra sweaters to give him that muscle-bound Travolta look. The girls fell for it, and for a while Paco was king of the disco.

Unfortunately he was so popular that he would be dancing late into the night and, with all those sweaters, he started losing even more weight. The thinner he got, the more he had to wear to keep up his image.

He finally collapsed while boogying with a blonde. Doctors had to remove a jacket and nine sweaters before they could treat him for heat stroke.

MOST OVER-RATED ROMEOS

The descendants of Casanova and Romeo hardly live up to the reputation of their race, according to a recent survey.

The 400-page report entitled *The Sexual Behaviour of Italians* reveals that 24 per cent of Italian wives consider their husbands totally inadequate in bed and 48 per cent only pretend to be satisfied when their husbands made love to them.

KEENEST MEMBER OF PLAID CYMRU

In 1970 *Private Eye* discovered this letter to a local paper:

'Dear Sir,

I am not a Welsh teacher, but love my country very dearly. Learning Welsh at school did me no harm, as I received equal marks in both languages, Welsh and English (full marks).

I think that Welsh is far more pleasant and useful than sex, of which people seem to get so much these days.

J Jones
Caergytli
Sir Fou'

LEAST URGENT EMERGENCY

Police in Munich who received a call on the emergency line were convinced that they were listening to a murder. Down the line came the sound of a woman clearly in distress, crying, 'No, no – help!' followed by the sound of scuffling.

They traced the call and two patrol cars dashed round to the address, sirens blaring. A team of policemen burst the door down – and found a couple making love on the sofa. On the floor nearby was the telephone, off the hook.

Unamused, the police prosecuted the couple for misuse of the emergency services. It emerged in court that the call had been made unintentionally at the height of passion.

An embarrassed Gertrude Schuler explained, 'I must have pushed the buttons with my feet.'

Case dismissed.

MOST CONTAGIOUS COUNTRY

In Vietnam during the mid-1970s, an average of more than 40,000 cases of venereal disease were being reported every week.

LEAST ROMANTIC LADY
OF THE LAKE

A sixty-three year old Bulgarian man could scarcely believe his luck when walking along the deserted beach of a lake. There, just offshore, was a rowing boat, in which an attractive blonde woman sat, beckoning him to climb on board.

'I knew what she had in mind,' he said later. 'She had the bottom part of her bikini tied to an oar.'

But after they had rowed out to the middle of the lake and made love, the woman demanded £9. When the man refused, she started to rock the boat and threatened to pull the plug out. He couldn't swim so he paid up quickly.

After she had asked for several similar offences to be taken into consideration, the woman was jailed for three months.

STRONGEST REASON FOR NOT
REACHING PUBERTY IN NEW GUINEA

The Marind-Anim tribe of New Guinea are reported to celebrate the arrival of particular boys at the age of puberty with spectacular rites.

A sexual orgy takes place for several days and nights in which everyone in the village makes love to one another – except the initiate.

On the final night, amid drums and ecstatic celebrations, a young girl is brought out, painted and perfumed, into the middle of the dancing ground where she is lain beneath a platform of very heavy logs. The boy then comes out and has to make love to her in front of the tribe. As he does, the supports of the platform are pulled away.

The bodies of the crushed couple are chopped up, roasted and ceremoniously eaten by the rest of the tribe.

MOST FREQUENTLY DISCARDED HABITS

In a survey, conducted by Father Silvano Burgalassi among thousands of Italian priests and nuns, over one third of those interviewed admitted breaking their vows of chastity.

LEAST POPULAR SEXUAL POSITION

Mademoiselle Bompard, an adventurous young Frenchwoman who lived in the nineteenth century had something of a problem. She had two lovers, and she really only wanted one.

Her solution to the problem was tortuous but effective.

She invited her first lover, a Monsieur Gouffe, to her room where, as part of an erotic game, she persuaded him to sit by a curtain in front of an alcove. Then she sat on his knee and playfully put a rope made of silk around his neck.

Monsieur Gouffe found this loveplay engaging until he was jerked up into the air and hung by the noose from a pulley on the ceiling until he was dead.

Hidden behind the curtain had been Mademoiselle Bompard's second lover, Monsieur Eyraud. She had passed the rope to him and, with a quick tug, it was curtains for Gouffe.

LEAST LADYLIKE PERSONAL AD

An unusually frank advertisement recently appeared in *The Lady* magazine:

YOUNG ITALIAN COUPLE seek Nanny Au Pair, one year minimum, for baby one year. Also English conversation. Good relaxed family atmosphere, no housework or cocking.

DOTTIEST CASE OF PERMISSIVENESS

At the height of the sexual revolution of the late 1960s, the adventurous Dutch Provo group came up with a novel suggestion.

In order to avoid social stigma and the fear of penetration, doctors should be required to remove hymens on request.

LEAST POPULAR SEX CLUB
IN THE WORLD

One of the worst fates that can befall a young boy in India is to be sent to the local eunuch colony.

There are an estimated one million eunuchs in India, and they find their recruits from families who fear for some reason that their child is sexually abnormal or malformed. It has also been widely reported that the eunuchs lure adolescent boys into their communities and sometimes resort to kidnapping.

The children are gradually converted to the ways of the group and then, at puberty, the grisly and often fatal castration is done by a eunuch 'surgeon'.

A superstitious fear of the eunuchs, and a moral disapproval of their links with homosexuality, means that they are outcasts from Indian society.

But help may be on the way. Kraita Lal Bhola, a salesman for motor-scooter spares in New Delhi is mounting a campaign to rehabilitate the eunuchs. He has already petitioned world leaders, including the Queen.

'Cannot Queen Elizabeth intervene for the eunuchs?' pleads his latest press release.

MOST COMPREHENSIVE POLICE STATEMENT

After a 26-year-old woman had made a statement at the police station at Ndola, Zambia, Constable Phiri asked her if she would make love to him and offered her ten shillings.

She refused. He offered her fifteen shillings and she agreed.

Phiri then took her upstairs to a lecture hall where they both took their clothes off and started making love on the floor.

At a critical moment, the door opened and Assistant Commissioner Humphrey Nthere of the Zambian CID entered with a group of police trainees. He asked the constable what he thought he was doing.

Without looking up, Phiri replied that he was very busy taking a statement. Would they please come back in ten minutes?

'As far as I know there is no rule against fornication in the station,' he later told a magistrate. 'I removed my uniform out of respect.'

BIZARREST FRIENDSHIP

'My intensive karate training has made me impotent, and not even a beautiful young virgin could arouse me,' karate champion Yunitso Ato told a Munich court, when accused of rape. 'Please bring on a young sexy woman and I will prove it here in front of everyone.'

A 26-year-old waitress claimed that she had been making love with her boyfriend when Yunitso, a friend of theirs, came in and asked whether he could take over. The boyfriend not only complied but held her down while Yunitso raped her.

When the judge expressed puzzlement at the boyfriend's behaviour, the girl explained, 'He obeyed Yunitso in everything'.

The karate champion's version was different. He said, 'I came into the room by chance. She was in bed naked, completely indifferent to my friend's love-making. I gave her a cigarette and kissed her knee to stir her passions.'

When he was found guilty and the judge sentenced him to two years' jail, Yunitso jumped up, taking a martial arts stance, and had to be restrained.

SHORTEST LIVED ELOPEMENT

After Achilles Thistos, aged 96, had forbidden his sister Constantina, aged 76, to marry her fiance Tantos Diamantopulo, aged 84, the spirited couple decided to elope one night.

Unfortunately they were interrupted by Achilles. Tantos fell off the ladder and broke his leg and Achilles tripped over him breaking his ankle.

Constantina was unhurt.

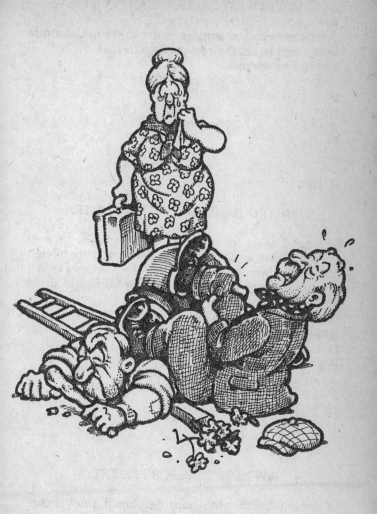

MELLOWEST CALIFORNIAN COUPLES

Over two thousand couples under thirty in California were asked to list their favourite activities.

Sex came seventh.

MOST DOUBLE-EDGED HOSPITALITY

The good news for guests of the Tchuktchi tribe in Siberia is that, as a sign of hospitality, you are offered one of their women for the night. The bad news is that you are first presented with a bowl of the girl's urine with which to wipe out your mouth.

If you refuse it, you are considered an enemy of the family and are thrown out into the cold.

BATTIEST CURE FOR FRIGIDITY

In ancient China, physicians developed a novel cure for frigidity. They would capture a particular species of red bat, kill it, grind it into a powder and rub it all over the frigid woman's body.

MOST DOCTRINALLY CORRECT ATTITUDE OF THE INDUSTRIALIZED URBANIZED PROLETARIAT WHEN FACED WITH PETIT BOURGEOIS REVISIONISM TOWARDS THE FINAL COLLAPSE OF WESTERN MONOPOLY CAPITALISM (IN THE BEDROOM)

It was in 1973 that Aldo Brandirali, Secretary-General of the Italian Marxist-Leninist Party, announced some grave news for the comrades. He said:

'Sex without class-consciousness cannot give satisfaction even if it is repeated until infinity.'

SEVEN

PUBLIC FACES, PRIVATE FLOPS

'So we had an affair. You must be pretty bad – I can't even remember you.'

Bianca Jagger to Warren Beatty

LEAST SYMPATHETIC STAR

Robert Savage, a good-looking millionaire's son, made a serious mistake when he fell in love with the Hollywood sex goddess of the twenties, Clara Bow.

He was, it appears, almost the only man in America not to have heard of the actress' phenomenal sexual appetite. At her peak, Miss Bow had made love to most of Hollywood's leading men, athletes, stuntmen, extras and, according to one rumour, the entire University of Southern California football team (thus coining the expression 'bow-legged').

Savage took it in bad part when he discovered that, where Clara Bow was concerned, he was not playing the starring role. He tried to slash his wrist, letting the blood flow on to a portrait of his loved one.

Clara was unimpressed. 'Jesus Christ, he's got to be kidding,' she said. 'Men don't slash wrists, they use a gun!'

MOST DIFFICULT TO PLEASE
FILM STAR

After the inevitable Victorian upbringing, Dyan Cannon has written that she was overcome by guilt after indulging in teenage cuddling sessions on her parents' settee. She took up religion instead and remained pure for 'five or six years'.

Then Cary Grant provided some momentary relief. 'He was serious about me from the beginning,' says Dyan. 'After we got married I learned to trust him and gradually came to understand what orgasm meant.'

Unfortunately, having made this discovery, the star

101

had a relapse. 'I shut down again. I felt too good, so I thought there must have been something wrong.'

Cary and Dyan got divorced.

SLOWEST BEGINNER

Clarinettist Artie Shaw claimed that he first slept with a girl in his teens, but only because the other members of his band would tease him mercilessly about being a virgin. For peace rather than love, he gave in and surrendered his virginity.

However he warmed up after this slow start. He has so far been married eight times, and his wives include Ava Gardner and Lana Turner.

PHONIEST MOMENT OF ECSTASY

With its come-on title, flashes of nudity and, above all, its steamy scenes, Hedy Lamarr's first film *Ecstasy* enjoyed a *succès de scandale* for years. Indeed, when she got married in 1933, Lamarr's husband Fritz Mandl spent a fortune trying to buy up all the prints of the film – without success.

But those exotic scenes were distinctly phony. In order to introduce a little passion into the proceedings, the director Gustav Machatý stood just off camera holding a pin which he would stick into his leading lady's bum at the critical moment.

As the cameras rolled and Hedy writhed, another Hollywood legend was born.

LEAST EASY TO ENGAGE IN AGREEABLE CONVERSATION

In the forefront of the modish dislike of all things sexual is Toyah Wilcox.

'I hate the whole sex scene,' she says. 'I'd put a bottle over the head of anybody who tried to chat me up.'

CLUMSIEST CONTENDER

Moody but magnificent Marlon Brando has considerably less than meets the eye on screen, according to his ex-wife Anna Kashfi, who wrote an entire book on Marlon's failings.

He was a 'clumsy lover', she claimed, and less than well endowed. 'To be honest, the great Brando is not so great in bed.'

SADDEST FATHER CONFESSOR

In the great tradition of Hollywood sex symbols, Jean Harlow had a truly terrible sex life. After a disastrous first marriage, she apparently resisted all overtures from the studs and stars of Glitter City. Then she met Paul Bern, a 40-year-old producer who, by all accounts, was as near to the perfect nine-stone weakling as has ever had sand kicked in his face.

None of that would have mattered too much since it appears that Harlow was pleased to find a man interested in her rather than her body and Bern appeared to be a kind man — indeed he had been nicknamed 'Hollywood's Father Confessor' because many of the female stars would confide in him.

Unfortunately he had other problems. On their wedding night, Harlow rang her agent Arthur Landau up and asked him to collect her. She revealed that Bern had beaten her with a cane and had bitten her thighs brutally and drawn blood.

The next morning, Landau went round to the house and found the bridegroom in tears. 'Every man I know gets an erection just by talking about her,' he said. 'Didn't I have the right to think Jean could help me that much?'

Later it was to emerge that Bern was totally impotent and had the sexual organs of a small boy. The marriage continued after a fashion for months, until one night Bern burst into their bedroom with a gigantic false penis. Later it was flushed down the lavatory.

'Hollywood's Father Confessor' was found dead the next day. The last words of his suicide note to Jean Harlow were, 'You understand that last night was only a comedy.'

MOST FREQUENTLY DISAPPOINTING
STAR LOVER

In a moment of utter frankness Gitty Milinaire spoke of her all-too-brief affair with Omar Sharif.

'I did not enjoy our lovemaking,' she said 'and once was enough.'

Omar was also given a bad press by Barbara Streisand who, also overcome by utter frankness, confided to the world's press that he was always in a hurry and talked incessantly about bridge.

COOLEST REBUFF

When Ryan O'Neal met Oona Chaplin, he was captivated and soon after wrote to her, asking her to live with him.

'How flattering,' Oona is reputed to have said, 'but I don't go out with little boys.'

She was later seen in the company of David Bowie.

SINATRA'S SMALL DISAPPOINTMENT

An article in *Vice-Roi* magazine revealed a little known aspect of the Hollywood star circuit.

Subtly headlined 'THE BIGGEST TOOL IN SHOWBIZ', it tells the breathtaking story of Roddy McDowall and how Roddy's 'massive hidden asset' made erotic failures of Tinsel Town's big boys:

It seems that most of the Hollywood he-men secretly pride themselves on being supermen when it comes to doing what counts.

So Frank Sinatra had all the great studs of Beverly Hills gathered in his mansion for an unofficial heavyweight contest.

Peter O'Toole, Dean Martin, Rock Hudson, Paul Newman, Robert Mitchum, Big John Wayne, Sammy Davis – they were all there. And so was Roddy.

One by one they dropped their pants and displayed their armaments. McDowall, who was at the end of the line, didn't even blink when he spied the formidable equipment that everybody from O'Toole to Caine were in the process of displaying.

When it was his turn, he quietly unzipped his trousers, folded back the double folds on his custom-made undies (the only kind he can wear for support, they cost him $20 a pair, and last a long time) and exposed an organ that could have served as an ICBM if the Defense Department fought its wars in bed.

'Amazing!' stammered Sinatra, who up till then thought he was the heftiest man around.

'Incredible!' gasped Peter O'Toole, whose reputation in Dublin had him pegged as a real winner when it came to doing what counts.

'Wow!' freaked Rock Hudson, who couldn't get his eyes back into their sockets.

But that's the story of easy-going Roddy McDowall's action-packed life.

On top of all that, he's one of the best actors Hollywood has ever seen, a formidable photographer, and an all round likeable chap.

The reporter did not reveal the source for his story.

MOST JADED CONFESSION

Robin Askwith, star of the famous *Confession* films, was surrounded by beautiful women on and off the set. But all was not as it seemed.

'I'm probably the lousiest real-life lover in show business today,' he told the *News of the World*. 'It's true in my early days I ploughed through God knows how many women but, after a while, it has an odd effect on you. After you have been at it all day, you don't much feel like getting out there and doing it again at night.'

DREAMIEST FLASHER

The simulation of sex acts on stage by rock stars has been part of showbiz ever since Elvis first waggled his pelvis, but some of the wildest practitioners of the act are, like the King, no longer with us.

Jimi Hendrix was famous for what he did to his guitar on stage and in 1969 Jim Morrison, legendary lead singer of The Doors, went a stage further, exposing himself on stage in a moment of over-excitement.

The fans loved it, but the police didn't and later arrested him. Jim's famous words on this occasion were, 'Uh-oh. I think I exposed myself out there.'

BUNNIES' WORST BUCK

When Shirley Hillman, Hugh Hefner's social secretary revealed the secrets of the playboy millionaire's lifestyle, she was rather less than complimentary about some of his guests.

Surrounded by attractive Playboy bunnies, Ryan O'Neal behaved like a hillbilly, Sammy Davis Jnr. made a lot of noise ('he was always dancing round, clicking his fingers and jangling the jewellery he wore') and Linda Lovelace was a 'thin, depressed-looking woman with stringy, mousy hair'.

But the greatest disappointment was Tom Jones.

'When he walked through the door, they expected a tall, virile superstud, full of whimsical Welsh charm. Instead this tongue-tied little man arrived.'

After this inauspicious entry, Tom 'took advantage' of a lot of girls but none of them, said Shirley, was at all impressed with his performance as a lover.

LEAST WELCOME
EARLY MORNING CALL

'I remember the first time I saw Kenny with his shirt off,' Lee Everett confided to a Sunday newspaper, 'I thought "God, he's bony". He looked like a new-born Great Dane.'

But despite this unpromising first impression, Kenny Everett and Lee finally achieved union after going out together for a year. It was apparently something of a turn-up for Lee.

'We were very drugged at the time and it just happened, much to our surprise and amazement. It was lovely. The next thing we did was to ring up all our friends in the small hours and tell them all about it. And then we went out to celebrate.'

'There's nothing wrong with our marriage. I'd put it up against anybody's.'

The couple separated a few months later.

DOTTIEST HOLLYWOOD BEHAVIOUR

The disaster-prone erotic life of Joan Crawford has been well-documented, above all by her daughter Christina, but one peculiar Crawford habit has rarely been recorded.

After each one of her four marriages, she would rename her house in Hollywood. She would also change all the lavatory seats.

MOST SURPRISING SEXUAL REMINISCENCE

Relaxing in sequins and make-up, family entertainer Liberace enjoys telling the story of the day he lost his virginity. It turns out to be something of a surprise.

'I think I was raped . . . she was a big, chesty broad who sang blues songs . . . All of a sudden this hand started coming up my leg and she said, "Oh, you're a big boy, aren't you?" Then she took it out and started gobbling it . . . Then she crawled over on my lap and screwed me.'

The experience apparently left something of an impression on the legendary artiste.

'And oh, God,' he said, 'I had lipstick all *over* my white pants!'

MOST CELEBRATED PROFESSIONAL VIRGIN

'Needless to say, I was a virgin when I married, like my mother before her, and her mother before her . . . and I've raised my daughter the same way.'

And, needless to say, the speaker was Hollywood's answer to the permissive society, Debbie Reynolds.

Debbie was defending her virtue from an early age – she started a Non-Neckers Club at high school – and, by the time she met Eddie Fisher, she didn't even know what French kissing was. She went on to marry him and to build a career based on her professional virgin image.

These days, all that Debbie will say about life after lights out with Eddie was that it was 'not unpleasant'.

ODDEST HOLLYWOOD SCENE

Shortly after Linda Lovelace became the most famous porno star in the world, she and her oafish husband/manager, Chuck Traynor, struck up a friendship with Sammy Davis Jnr.

'Are you into scenes?' Sammy asked one night.

Soon Linda was involved in frequent scenes with Sammy. But he was always a perfect gentleman.

'He had his own code of marital fidelity,' Linda wrote later. 'He explained to me that he could do anything except have normal intercourse because that, the act of making love, would be cheating his wife. What he wanted me to do, then, was to deep-throat him. Because that would not be an act of infidelity.'

This agreeable relationship continued until one night Sammy, Chuck and Linda were enjoying a normal quiet evening at Sammy's house – the two guys were watching a porno movie while Linda gave Sammy a blow-job – when their host asked Linda about her oral technique. He'd really like to try it out on someone.

According to Linda, it was now that she put into action her most enjoyable act of revenge on her brutal manager.

Chuck had a particular revulsion to any kind of homosexuality, being a quintessentially macho male and sexually insecure into the bargain. But he was so engrossed in the porn on the screen that he did not hear Linda tell Sammy that Chuck would just *love* to help him with the lesson – that it was just his sort of scene.

So, under cover of darkness, she moved over to Chuck but, as she put it, 'I was the one who unzipped his trousers, but I wasn't the one who knelt in front of him.'

It was several minutes before he realized what the star was up to and then, panic and disgust all over his face, he beckoned to Linda to come over and help him. She laughed and shook her head. Because Chuck was terrified of alienating his famous friend, he suffered in silence for several more minutes.

JUST LIKE A WOMAN

In a shock exclusive, Dana Gillespie told a Sunday newspaper about her brief affair with Bob Dylan. According to Dana, he was more impressive on stage than off it.

'When it came to the loving stakes, he was not terribly good,' said Dana candidly. 'I think he just wanted someone voluptuous to cuddle. I was a substitute teddy-bear.'

MICK'S LEAST SUCCESSFUL SEDUCTION

It wasn't that Playboy owner Hugh Hefner's houses in Chicago and California were whorehouses – more that famous people used to come and stay and Playboy bunnies were made available to them.

Hefner himself regarded women of twenty-four as being sexually over the hill and avoided talking to all but his closest entourage.

During the Rolling Stones' tour of America, he invited the entire group to his house in Chicago where soon, in true rock star fashion, a poolside orgy was in full swing.

But while the boys chased bunnies, Mick Jagger had taken a fancy to Hugh Hefner's ex-mistress Bobby Arnstein. Bobby had just finished lunch in her room when a dishevelled Mick staggered and lurched towards her. Bobbie pushed him away, the star staggered and sat down – on a large chocolate cake that was still on the lunch tray.

Mortified at the sight of his skintight white trousers

covered in chocolate, Mick hobbled out of the room and back to his hotel.

WHACKIEST DEFLORATION

According to Jack Lemmon, his introduction to sex was a wild affair.

Jack was a nervous teenager but one night, after several beers, he borrowed a friend's car, parked it in a quiet square and escorted his girlfriend to it.

Five minutes later, with one foot caught on the gear-shift and the other having torn a hole in the canvas roof of the car, Jack was no longer a virgin. He was also in such contortions that he was gasping with pain. His girlfriend, assuming that he was in ecstasies, responded with screams of encouragement. At that moment, the enraged owner of the car arrived.

Film rights in this scene have not yet been sold.

LEAST CONVINCING HARD LUCK STORY

Sultry sex symbol Omar Sharif has made a disappointing and touching confession. 'I have to fight for my girlfriends,' he says. 'I have to work much harder than anyone else.'

114

SLIGHTLY OFF-KEY JAZZ GREAT

Duke Ellington led such an active and varied sex life that few would call him an erotic failure. He did however have one peculiarity, according to his son Mercer.

'He never seemed to be interested in the perfect woman. If she had a scar, or was slightly misproportioned – big-busted, big-hipped or a little off-balance – then he was more interested.'

MOST BASHFUL SAILOR

Diana Dors has recently told the story of round-the-world yachtsman Chay Blyth's attempt at seducing her.

According to Diana, the intrepid sailor was staying in a hotel near a Northern club at which Diana was appearing. He had taken a fancy to her but, instead of approaching Britain's blonde bombshell himself, sent her two henchmen to bring her to his hotel room.

She told them to haul anchor.

EIGHT

THE NICEST VICES

'They set him on the flogging block,
They set him on his knee;
And the flush on his face and the
  flush on his bum
Was a stunning sight to see . . .'

Algernon Swinburne

MOST UNDERESTIMATED TYPE
OF FOREPLAY

The nineteenth-century writer Thomas Bartholinus revealed that England's pride of place as a world leader in the use of the rod for sexual pleasure was far from secure. All over the world, husbands were in the habit of knocking hell out of their wives as a loving preliminary to marital bliss. For example:

'Persians and Russians chastise their wives with blows from a stick on the posterior before they perform their marital duty. Barclay assures us that with the Russians the love of the husband is measured by the number of blows he gives. The bride in Russia would rather be without any other piece of household goods than rods.'

MOST DISCIPLINED ROADSIDE CAFE

Whenever Christopher Dearman, proprietor of the Castle Café in Newark, found money short in the till, he would take disciplinary action on his three sixteen-year-old waitresses by caning their bottoms.

Then one of them reported him to the police and the case was brought to court.

Giving evidence, Mr Dearman said, 'We were caning away for the best part of a year. Sometimes I did it, sometimes my wife. There were no complaints until Elaine Clarke was caned twice in one week.'

Mr and Mrs Dearman were fined £100.

MOST SELF-ABUSING SAINT

St Mary Marie Alacoque took her religious devotion to extreme lengths. She cut the name 'Jesus' into her chest and, because the scars did not last long enough, burnt them into her flesh.

She once wrote that, when she needed to clean up the vomit of a sick patient, she 'could not resist' doing so with her tongue.

She enjoyed it so much, she wished she could do it every day.

MOST LIMITED SADIST

In that great generation of sado-masochistic weirdos, one of the best known perverts was Frederick Hankey.

Having settled in Paris in 1840, he immersed himself in the world of pornography, prostitution and bizarre sexual activities. He boasted that he was a practising sadist and the pride of his pornographic collection were volumes of De Sade's *Justine* and his friend R. M. Milnes' epic flagellant poem *The Rodiad*.

Hankey's greatest fantasy and ambition was described by Milnes as an 'extreme desire to see a girl hanged and have the skin of her backside tanned to bind his *Justine* with'.

Mentioned in the Goucourt diaries as one of the English aristocrats 'who bring ferocious cruelty to love and whose licentiousness can only be aroused by the woman's sufferings', Hankey tells the diarists that he likes to visit a brothel which provided facilities for flogging girls from thirteen upwards: 'We could also stick needles into them, not very long needles – only as long as this – and he showed us the tip of his finger.'

His skin fantasy preoccupied him throughout his life but *Justine* remained in its traditional binding, despite efforts by Hankey's friend Sir Richard Burton to find him the skin of a negress during his travels in Africa.

'I have been here three days,' Burton wrote to Milnes in 1863, 'and am generally disappointed. Not a woman killed, not a fellow tortured. The canoe floating in blood is a myth of myths. Poor Hankey must still wait for his *peau de femme*.'

But even Hankey's erotic tastes were something of a disappointment to Burton.

'There is no accounting for tastes in superstition,' he is reported by Milnes to have said, listing Hankey's perversions, 'yet he could not be persuaded to try the sensation of f . . .g a Muscovy duck while its head was cut off.'

MOST RIDICULOUS PUBLIC OUTRAGE

The life of many schoolmasters at prep schools and public schools has been impoverished by the growing concern about the effects on both parties of caning, birching and other corporal punishment.

The rot can be seen to have set in late in the nineteenth century when liberals, freethinkers and other wets began to write to *The Times* questioning whether beating up small boys was in the best interest of education.

One of the earliest whiners was a Mr Lonsdale who, in 1874, complained that his son, a pupil at Shrewsbury, had been over-zealously punished by Mr Moss, the headmaster, for being found with a bottle of ale in his study. Mr Moss was outraged at the complaint.

After all, he had only given the boy eighty-eight strokes with the birch.

MOST ONE-SIDED SEXUAL RELATIONSHIP

There are few animals that have not at some time been the startled recipient of intimate human advances. Bestiality with dogs, sheep, cows, chickens and other domesticated animals is, of course, well documented.

More exotically, Roman women used to use the heads of live snakes for pleasure. Others have smeared honey on their vagina and derived satisfaction from flies or bees that gathered there. Then there is the insertion of goldfish epically described in Shirley Conran's novel *Lace*.

The oddest and one of the most unpleasant partnerships on record is the story of the man who would pluck the wings off a fly and leave it struggling miserably on the end of his penis, providing him with an unforgettable *frisson*.

WETTEST FETISH

An unusual type of sexual pleasure has recently been revealed by a *Forum* reader. She likes to pee in her pants – particularly when she has just seen someone else getting soaked to the skin.

She goes on to recount an incident when, sitting at a canal-side café, she saw someone fall out of a boat.

'Whether it was because the woman was wearing my favourite colour and type of nylon panties, I don't know, but although my bladder was nowhere near full, I became extremely tense. I could think of nothing else but wetting my knickers and soaking my clothes like the woman who had just fallen into the water.'

Trembling with desire, the woman ordered another pot of tea and 'absolutely bursting' hurried along to one of the canal bridges. There she let go, wet her knickers and 'in a high state of erotic arousal' leapt into the canal.

MOST ENGLISH FORM OF EDUCATION

Flagellants will argue that to include the simple pleasure afforded by a good whacking as an erotic failure is unfair. But punishment of the involuntary kind that is still prevalent at boarding schools is worth including.

One of the best accounts of the effect of habitual beatings at an early age is in *The Autobiography of an Englishman* by 'Y', which was published in 1975.

'Y' was beaten by his father quite a bit but it was his prep school Newton Lodge which implanted in him a lifelong obsession with flagellation.

The school captain, aged fourteen, was something of

an expert at the art and used to beat the younger boys regularly and as a matter of course. There was also the all-important element of ritual:

'In the big schoolroom there were high sash windows, raised or lowered by means of thin, hard bind cord. It was an amusement to the prefects to make smaller boys bend over the window sill and lay their heads beneath the open window in the manner of one on the execution block. Then the window was gently lowered, and the boy was whipped on the bottom with the bind cord.'

With a headmaster who was also a devoted beater, 'Y' was soon hooked, particularly on the showing of weals on the bottom to other boys which inevitably followed punishment.

It was, he wrote, 'one of the keenest pleasures known to schoolboys'.

MOST ENTHUSIASTIC ANIMAL LOVERS

The alternative press's own agony uncle Dr Eugene Schoenfeld, alias Dr Hip Occrates, used to receive a steady stream of letters from potential bestialists.

'My wife and I think it might be interesting for her to have intercourse, regularly, with a German shepherd dog,' wrote one man, worried about 'the weird diseases one might get'.

The hip doctor warned them about intestinal worms. He was more sympathetic to the man who confided that he had 'fantasies of balling a female gorilla or other large ape . . . This is not a put on!'

Dr Hip Occrates advised a trip to the zoo to swot up on ape sexual techniques.

SWEATIEST RUBBERIST

Celebrated in the glossy magazines and patronized by pop stars like Kim Wilde, London's Skin 2 Club became in 1983 the acceptable face of fetishism.

One of their clients – or rubberists, as they like to be called – explained his tastes to Fiona Russell Powell of *The Face*: 'I'd like to be encased in rubber from head to foot with no eye slits or mouth slits, just a nose-hole to let me breathe. Then I would lie down in a rubber-lined coffin, have the lid closed and padlocked over me and left for two or three days. I think I'd just go crazy!'

But rubberism does have its practical snags.

'While we've been chatting,' writes Fiona, 'the legs of David's suit have billowed up to the knee. I thought it was trapped air at first but soon found out I was wrong. "I must be squelching around in about two pints of sweat", he laughs.'

MOST EXTREME CASE OF BONDAGE

A musician called Kotzwarra enjoyed various bizarre sado-masochistic practices.

When he asked a prostitute called Susanna Hill to split his genitals in two, she demurred, but finally agreed to string him up while she went out to attend to other clients.

She had such a busy night that it was several hours before she returned, by which time Kotzwarra had died of suffocation.

SWISHEST DINNER PARTY

The natural affection many English men and women have for smacking, birching, getting beaten up and other forms of 'discipline' is well known but one occasion when *'le vice anglais'* was taken rather too far was a dinner party in Yorkshire that took place late in the eighteenth century. The evening was later described by an anonymous author. The host was a keen flagellant, as were his three guests.

'On going into the dining room, they met with a remarkable sight. In the four corners of the room were four candelabras, apparently held by four boys with naked posteriors. They were tied up, and the hands so fastened that it looked as if they held the candelabra. After the first course the four worthy pedagogues set themselves to flogging the bare posteriors of the boys, in which work Dr S. and the host were the most zealous.'

After four boys brought in the dessert, the host took out 'four beautiful little canes bound with blue ribbon' and the quartet returned to the fray.

After supper, one of the guests, Mr J, was strapped on to a specially constructed 'horse' and was punished by his friends. They were hugely amused by his screams.

'Mr J roared with pain and begged to be let loose which, however, did not disturb the second Dr Keate in his favourite occupation. Dr S continued the flagellation of his colleague, till the poor Mr J, half fainting with pain, was set free.'

The evening ended with a hand of whist.

LEAST ENDEARING PARTY TRICK

A wormlike amphibian called the caecilian enjoys a
sexual habit that has not yet been emulated by the
human species. When aroused, the male pushes out
the wall of its anus to form a long pointed cone which
it thrusts deep into the anus of its mate.

LEAST CONVINCING CONTRIBUTION TO
THE WOMEN'S MOVEMENT

When Sidney Perks was arrested by a policewoman
for walking down Florence Nightingale Walk dressed
as a nun, he had an immediate explanation.

He said that his girlfriend was a feminist and had
threatened to leave him unless he discovered what it
was like to be a woman.

WEIRDEST WEIRDOS

There's something particularly English about some of
the stranger requests reported by prostitutes in Wayland Young's book *Eros Denied*.

One of them had a client who made her stand naked
while he threw kippers wrapped in cellophane at her.
Another punter liked the girl to sit with her legs apart
on the other side of the room. Then he'd take some
cream buns out of a paper bag and throw them at her

('Not a bad shot he was either, once he'd got his aim,' she said). Afterwards, he would cover her in marmalade, put iced cherries up her and tuck in.

Not all the erotic failures were that exotic. One man enjoyed the more predictable pleasure of being manacled down and having hot wax poured on his member.

He was an MP, of course.

LEAST POPULAR SPANKER

A curiously English criminal roamed the streets of London in 1680. His name was Whipping Tom.

Whipping Tom was a sort of roving flagellant who for several months made life quite impossible for women of all classes in the Holborn area.

According to a contemporary account, he would lurk in alleys and 'at unawares seizes upon such as he can conveniently light on, and turning them up as nimble as an Eel, makes their Butt ends cry Spanko; and then (according to the report of those who have felt the weight of his Paws) vanished.'

Whipping Tom was never unmasked.

WORST CASE OF GETTING THE ELBA

Elly was a broad-minded woman. When her husband Oscar came to bed on their wedding night in the full regalia of the Emperor Napoleon, she was only slightly taken aback and let him make love to her if he agreed to take off the thigh-length boots and three-cornered hat.

But after four years of being chafed by the Napoleonic uniform and medals every time they made love, Elly decided that this had gone on long enough and asked him to take it off.

Oscar not only refused, but immediately sued for divorce.

MOST INCORRIGIBLE MP

Undoubted heroine of London's flagellomaniacs in the early part of the nineteenth century was Mrs Theresa Berkley, for whom the whip provided a vast fortune.

Mrs Berkley's establishment off Portland Place provided every form of sado-masochistic enjoyment that her male clientele could dream of. She had a huge variety of whips, cats, thongs, and contraptions so that, as a contemporary writer put it, 'in her establishment, anyone provided with reasonable means could have himself beaten with canes, scourges, whips and straps, pricked with needles, half-strangled, scrubbed with many kinds of harsh brushes, scourged with nettles, curry-combed, bled and tortured until he had enough of it.'

To this end, Mrs Berkley invented the famous 'Berkley Horse' or 'chevalet', an apparatus for flogging

men which allowed only the head and genitals room for movement. It was a wild success and masochists travelled across Europe to be flogged in it.

Unfortunately, there were among Mrs Berkley's clients, men whose need for punishment was so extreme that they can only be regarded as erotic failures. One, an MP who introduced himself as 'an ill-behaved young man and quite incorrigible', wrote to her with specific instructions:

1. It is necessary that I should be securely fastened to the Chevalet with chains which I will bring myself.
2. A pound sterling for the first blood drawn.
3. Two pounds sterling if the blood runs down to my heels.
4. Three pounds sterling if my heels are bathed in blood.
5. Four pounds sterling if the blood reaches the floor.
6. Five pounds sterling if you succeed in making me lose consciousness.

LAMEST EXCUSE

In a letter to *Forum* magazine, Mr S. L. of Arizona revealed that he can only make love to women with a limp – 'not amputees or any weird stuff like that', he says. They just have to be slightly lame.

He goes on to tell the unhappy story of his affair with a lovely young thing who had sprained her ankle playing tennis. But then, disaster struck.

'The first time I saw her without her little support

bandage, I got very nervous. She walked a few steps and proudly announced, "See? No limp!" Well, was she ever wrong, there was plenty limp. I couldn't get an erection for her, no matter how I tried.'

Later she limped around the apartment for him but it just wasn't the same.

GAMIEST AUSTRALIAN PUNTER

The woman that claimed David Niven's virginity was a prostitute called Nessie.

Nessie normally used to avoid what she called 'specials' but occasionally used to go along with seven other girls to the flat of an Australian millionaire with a somewhat peculiar fetish.

He would get the girls to undress and, as he walked around crowing like a cockerel, the girls were required to push pheasants' feathers up his bum. The most exciting moment in the proceedings would be when the Australian, now with a full tail of feathers, threw some corn on the floor.

As his 'hens' scrabbled about for it in a circle around him, the 'cockerel' would noisily reach his climax.

MOST UNNERVING HOST

Never popular among his more straight-laced contemporaries, Algernon Swinburne was described by John Ruskin as 'standing up to his neck in a cesspool, and adding to its contents'.

Having, like so many others, been introduced to the joy of pain by being flogged at Eton, he was a relentless flagellomaniac all his life. He also used to keep pet monkeys, with whom he appears to have had an unhealthy relationship.

On one occasion, a young man visited Swinburne who was accompanied by a monkey, dressed up in women's clothes. As Swinburne made sexual overtures to his guest, the monkey flew into a rage and attacked the visitor.

Later the man was persuaded to come back to have lunch with Swinburne. The main course was grilled monkey.

ROCKIEST LOVER

One of the greatest sexual highs a girl can have is to don a pair of boxing gloves and knock hell out of someone else, according to a recent letter to *Forum*.

Ms S. K. claims that, although she was never averse to a bit of 'rough stuff', it was a sexual rivalry between herself and a friend for the same man that turned her on to boxing. The girls put on a pair of gloves and sparred for a bit.

'We really enjoyed the physical pummelling,' says Ms S. K., adding regretfully, 'but the fight was no contest since I beat hell out of her, and we haven't been friends ever since.'

Encouraged by this experience, she now boxes with most of her male partners, although apparently some have expressed reservations, particularly since, as she puts it, 'I prefer a fight to finish where one party concedes defeat or is knocked out.'

Recently she has managed to KO two men who had taken her home.

'The sex I had with these men after beating them up was the most enjoyable and fulfilling I have ever experienced.'

When asked by Ms S. K. what they thought of it, both men said they found the experience 'very erotic'.

FRIENDLIEST FETISHIST

When a woman police constable entered a ladies' lavatory in Tring, she was confronted by a man dressed only in a black corset.

'When questioned,' the local paper reported, 'he admitted having been to the ladies' toilet, but he said he did not mean any harm, he was just being sociable.'

EARLIEST RECORDED AGE FOR
INCESTUOUS DESIRE

In his outspoken autobigriphy *Ruling Passions*, Tom Driberg – later Lord Bradwell – must lay strong claim to having the earliest awakenings of desire, albeit homosexual, on record:

'I was crawling about on the carpet in my father's study and cannot therefore have been more than two or three, when I found myself between the flannel-trousered legs of my brother, who was standing in the middle of the room talking. Looking up towards the crotch, I perceived a small hole – some stitches loose in the seam. Gently I inserted a finger – so gently that I don't think my brother noticed – and, though I did not quite touch flesh, I experienced what I clearly recall as the first authentic sexual thrill of my life.'

MOST ORIGINAL SIN

A letter to the well-known American advice columnist Dr Hip Occrates revealed an unusual problem:

Dear Doctor –

I am 45 years of age, unmarried and in excellent physical condition which I maintain by working out weekly at the YMCA. My problem is that every so often while doing chin-ups I have an orgasm. This prevents me from finishing my work-out but, after relaxing in the hot room, I seem to feel better than ever.

Nevertheless there are physical and moral implications I would like to have cleared up, i.e.:

1. Is this physically harmful?
2. Since I usually know it's going to happen and continue the chin-ups, anyway, would the Catholic church consider this masturbation and therefore a sin?

The doctor advised psychiatric guidance.

NINE

FEMALE TROUBLES

'A woman is a ship with two holes in her bottom.'

Olive Schreiner, Havelock Ellis' mistress

MOST HELPFUL WITNESS

When asked by a policeman whether she had any birthmarks, Mrs Austin of Hull immediately took down her trousers and pants.

Explaining her conduct to a court, Mrs Austin said she had no indecent intentions but regarded policemen as being asexual, like doctors.

MOST OFTEN DISAPPOINTED SUPERGROUPIE

Possibly Françoise Pascal's strongest claim to fame is as friend and comforter to famous males. But when she told all in a series of kiss-and-tell articles in a Sunday newspaper, sex among the glitterati was made to seem strangely boring.

Peter Sellers ('I only slept with him twice') was awkward, in and out of bed. Ilie Nastase farted a lot and worried about tennis ('It wasn't the greatest meeting of two bodies I've ever known'). And Warren Beatty was shy ('I was disappointed with our love-making ... he seems to freeze, which makes him pretty dull between the sheets.')

The articles did not reveal what the chaps thought of Françoise 'between the sheets'.

MOST FLAWED EXCUSE

When arrested for prostitution, Mrs Margaret Friend, aged forty-eight, of Southend-on-Sea, told a magistrate that she was too short-sighted to ply for trade, being blind in one eye and with only partial vision in the other.

'I can only see if someone is right on top of me,' she explained.

SILLIEST SEXUAL THEORY

For those looking for clues as to the sexual nature of women car owners, Dr Eric Trimmer has come up with the following model-by-model guide.

Sports Cars. Don't be fooled. 'Girls who drive sports cars often have subconscious problems of a homosexual nature . . . The tendency for role reversal is there and they are strong and domineering.'

Family Saloons. Another surprise. The car may be boring but the owner will be dynamite in bed. 'They really are very sexy,' says the doctor. 'They enjoy men and choose a car that comes second best to their own attractions.'

Estate Cars. Despite the room in the back, estate car owners are bad news apparently – particularly if there's a dog grill in the back.

Fun Cars. Zany little numbers with 'When I grow up, I want to be a Porsche' stickers and false panther-skin seat covers suggest a pathetic, exhibitionist streak in the owners and a low sex drive. Basically they're searching for a father figure.

LEAST KNOWN PATRIOTIC ACTIVITY

A High Court judge heard the expert opinion of Dr Archibald Jeffrey while judging a petition for damages from a woman who had lost her sexual appetite following a car crash. Dr Jeffrey told the court:

'Sexual intercourse is not a high wire act. Many women do not get satisfaction out of it. They do it for England.'

THINNEST RED LINE

In the heart of head-hunter country, the village of Karambaramba had little going for it. The men of the village were lousy fighters and ineffective hunters. As a result, they lost their territory and were, some years ago, facing disaster.

Finally, they came up with a solution. As soon as anyone threatened their village, the tribe would offer their womenfolk to the aggressors. It worked.

Now every woman in the village over the age of twelve is on the game and – while they keep working – the tribe is safe.

MOST FREQUENT TYPE OF FEMALE ORGASM

In the great clitoral versus vaginal versus G-Spot argument, it is sometimes forgotten that the most frequent type of female orgasm is the faked one.

In her exhaustive probe into female sexuality, Shere Hite did an orgasm survey among over 1600 women. Over fifty per cent were either regular fakers or had faked in the past.

MOST EXTREME FUNERAL BEHAVIOUR

According to Mariane Roalfe Cox's *An Introduction to Folk-Lore*, a custom still in practice in Fiji at the time of writing was the ritual strangling of a wife at the funeral of her husband.

NASTIEST FAMILY ROW

It was in 1974 that tragedy came to the Chettri family in Katmandu. The mother of the family Dhanamaya was raped by her thirty-six year old son, Narabahadur. She then beheaded him.

Appearing before the supreme court, Mrs Chettri was acquitted on the grounds that women had the legal right to kill a man so long as it is done within an hour of the offence.

144

LEAST SEDUCTIVE YONI

The *Kama Sutra* and *Auanga Ranga* list three types of
female sex organ, or *yoni*. The first is The Deer, small
and like the lotus-flower. Then there is The Mare,
rather larger but delicate. Finally, there is The Elephant,
which is twelve finger-breadths (about ten inches) in
length and smells like elephants in rut. Women with
these *yoni* are said by the sacred texts to have large
breasts, a broad face and short limbs. They are gluttonous,
eat noisily, have a loud and harsh voice and are
very difficult to satisfy sexually.

MOST RADICAL CURE FOR
FEMALE DESIRE

Sexual desire in females, long suspected by males as
being at best rather improper, was thought to be
particularly dangerous by doctors in seventeenth-
century France. There they maintained that such feelings in a woman were 'a melancholic affliction', probably suggesting serious mental illness, and took steps
to cure it.

One girl, who was found to be suffering seriously
from 'sexual excitement' after an affair with a servant,
was subjected by her doctor to a somewhat radical
course of no less than thirty bloodlettings.

A contemporary historian smugly reported that the
cure had utterly destroyed her 'mad love' and drawn
out her 'insane mind'. Unfortunately, it also killed her.

MOST EXTREME BRIDAL REQUEST

The men on Cook Island traditionally have to pass a rigorous virility test before being accepted as a husband.

The would-be bride would go for several days, and sometimes weeks, without washing her private parts. Then she will ask the man to perform cunnilingus before further intimacy is allowed.

KEENEST SUPPORTER OF LAW AND ORDER

When Mrs Charlotte Tyler, a nineteen year old housewife from Memphis, Tennessee appeared before a grand jury that was investigating a vice wave, she admitted that, over the past three years, she had made love to over 5,000 policemen of all ranks.

Asking to be released from her summons, Mrs Tyler explained that she was currently bringing an action for $1,000,000 against a health spa where, she said, she had been trapped in a sauna for one and a half hours. This experience had transformed her from a devout Catholic housewife into a raving nymphomaniac.

When asked about her penchant for policemen, she said, 'It may be something to do with my belief in law and order.'

MOST FERVENT SUPPORTER OF
BRITISH LEYLAND

Medical records are full of the various 'foreign bodies' discovered by doctors in patients' vaginas. They include goblets, hairpins, bottles, beerglasses and compasses.

One northern obstetric unit reported a particularly intriguing find: the gear knob of a British Leyland car.

UNRULIEST WOMAN

The excessive behaviour of Mary Combe, the wife of an innkeeper, in Somerset, has been quoted by historians as an example of a typical seventeenth-century 'unruly woman'.

Whether or not she would have regarded herself as an erotic failure, Mary certainly produced her share of embarrassments and failures in others.

Rampantly randy, Mary would, it was often complained by a male visitor to the inn, 'put her hand into his breeches to feel what he had', and then proclaim loudly that, 'if it were ready to stand she was ready for him'.

She would often try to seduce a man in front of his wife, would occasionally walk around the village in the nude and often, according to the records, 'layed down in the highway between Axbridge and Crosse, and called to all persons passing, by spreading her legs abroad, saying, "Come play with my cunt and make my husband a cuckold".'

In 1653, Mary threw a party which outraged local

parishioners. Only cuckolds and cuckold-makers, the outcasts of respectable society, were invited.

Although she may have gone a little far at times, Mary appears to have been popular in the village.

Or perhaps it was just that no one dared admit their distaste. People she disliked would sometimes awake to find their house spattered with human excrement.

It was Mary's calling card.

MOST UNEVEN LOVE MATCH

The female wheel-web spider is six hundred times heavier than the male, hundreds of whom live on her stomach to mate with her when required.

They are so small and insignificant that she hardly even bothers to eat them although, now and then, they provide her with a light snack.

LEAST TRAGIC KIDNAPPING

When fourteen women rebels in Morocco captured a thirty-year-old soldier called Hassan, they gave him specific duties. He was kept in a tent where he was ordered to be available to make love to each of the women.

By the time he was captured, eight of them were pregnant.

Hassan was taken straight to hospital suffering from extreme exhaustion.

MOST WORRIED WEIGHTWATCHER

An American alternative magazine's agony column has received the following letter:

'I am writing to you in regard to my weight problem. I am 22, 5' 6" tall and I weigh 134 pounds. I perform fellatio on my boyfriend an average four times a day. My girlfriend told me that the average calorific content of semen is 100. Is it true that I am gaining calories by injesting his semen? Should I add it to my calorie chart?'

The magazine advice was reassuring. Four times a day was perfectly all right, as long as she kept off sugar.

TEN

MEN AT WORK

'It was as a sucked gooseberry, a mere bit of dwindling flexible gristle.'

Frank Harris

MOST GENEROUS MALE LOVERS

The Malays of Borneo take their quest for sexual pleasure further than most. In order to improve the sensation for their lovers, some of the men perforate the penis with brass wire, bamboo, ivory, metal balls and anything else that comes to hand.

This selfless performance is rivalled by the Baltaks of Sumatra who cut the penis open and insert lumps of stone into the wounds so that, when it has healed, it produces a pleasant, gravelly sensation.

FASTER EVER SENSE OF HUMOUR LOSS

A man with something of a sense of fun, Klaus Rocher of Dusseldorf, bought for £187 a parrot called Lola whose party trick was, when asked, 'How was that?', to answer, 'Oh wonderful, WONDERFUL!'

Amusingly, he suspended the parrot's cage over his bed, to which he brought his latest girlfriend. After he had made love to her, he turned to Lola and asked expectantly, 'How was that?'

The parrot said nothing but let out a 'long cackle of ugly laughter'. When, to encourage her to perform, Klaus poked her, the parrot bit off his finger.

TACKIEST SOCIALITE

Ageing social butterfly Dai Llewelyn gave the *News of the World* a shock exclusive in 1980. His phobia about the noises girls make had lost him two lovers.

First to go was Isabelle Richli who, according to Dai, made a loud whistling noise as she slept.

Then there was Tessa Dahl. Apart from the problem of her size ('I mean she was a *big* girl,' said Gentleman Dai), she used to eat too noisily for him. On one occasion, he tape-recorded her eating breakfast and played the tape back to her at full volume.

The girls' opinion of the noises Dai makes was not revealed.

LEAST CONVINCING
ECCLESIASTICAL EXCUSE

Giving evidence against Father Bob Champain, a church charity raffle organizer in Steynings, PC Marcus Broadbent said, 'I was called to the new conveniences by Miss Gosport, a traffic warden. When I first saw Father Champain down on his knees I thought he was praying. Then I noticed that he was surrounded by a layer of brick and plaster chippings and that he was holding a stone hammer and a cold chisel.'

The Reverend Father, when asked about the incident at Steynings' Male and Female Lavatory Block, explained that he had just bought a Bumper Tool Kit and couldn't wait to get home to try it out.

LEAST SEXUAL SEX-WORSHIPPER

'Even if we can't act sexually,' wrote D. H. Lawrence, whose works are still a byword for a frank and earthy sexuality, 'let us at least think sexually, complete and clear.'

It appears that those words, rather than the wilder passages of *Lady Chatterley's Lover*, sum up the author's attitude to sex in his own life.

In print, he castigated the British for treating sex like a 'dirty, little secret'; in fact, he considered making love at any time except in the dark of night as being indecent. In print, he would attack the effete homosexuality of many of the literary establishment; in fact, he would talk of the 'blood brotherhood' of men and said that 'the nearest I have come to perfect love is with a young coal-miner when I was about sixteen'. In print, he wrote of his relationship with his wife Frieda that 'I hope to spend eternity with my face down-buried between her breasts'; in fact, the relationship was rather more complicated, and certainly more prosaic.

According to Dorothy Brett, who lived with them both, and who would have had an affair with Lawrence, had he been able to consummate their relationship, he had a brisk no-nonsense air about him which belies the mystical worship of the earth and the physical to be found in his writings.

One day in Mexico, the three of them were out riding together. Cantering along on a large grey horse, Frieda cried out in true Lawrentian fashion, 'Oh, it's wonderful: wonderful to feel his great thighs moving, to feel his powerful legs!'

'Rubbish,' said Lawrence grumpily, 'Don't talk like that. You've been reading my books: you don't feel anything of the sort!'

FULLEST DESCRIPTION OF A FLASHER

The *Crawley Observer* recently described a major local
news item as follows:

'A man indecently exposed himself to a twelve-year-
old girl in Grattans Park, Pound Hill, on Tuesday
evening last week. Police said he was about forty with
a black beard and short curly black hair, and short curly
black hair.'

CAMPEST DELEGATION

Fifty members of the Gay Liberation Front and the
Campaign for Sexual Equality invaded a British Medical Association Congress on sexual problems to protest
that they had not been invited to take part.

'We have the experience of being bullied all the
time,' said Bradford Gay Lib Spokesman Dan Milligan,
wearing a long blue slit-legged velvet dress with
sequins, tights, eye shadow, nail varnish and clogs.
'We don't like the way you talk about us as aberrant.'

LEAST APPETIZING SEXUAL SUBSTITUTE

An ex-prisoner has recently revealed why, in many
prisons, gardening duty is so popular among the
inmates.

Many of them collect worms and fill up a jam jar

156

with them. The result is apparently a much envied masturbatory device – not quite like the real thing but not at all bad.

MOST PERVERSE LAST SUPPER

It was in a brothel that one of the sons of Lord Milton earned himself a mention in social histories of the late eighteenth century.

One night, he went to one of the most fashionable brothels in London, asked for a large room and sent for twelve of the prettiest young girls. He gave them a sumptuous meal and afterwards made them undress and put on a licentious show for his pleasure. Then he paid them all handsomely and shot himself.

It was generally thought that his death showed great style.

MOST OVER-PUBLICISED
VICTORIAN GOOSEBERRY

Frank Harris, whose epic pornographic work *My Life and Loves* is generally regarded as being 90 per cent fantasy and 10 per cent fact, reveals one intimate moment which, temporarily at least, put him among the erotic failures.

During his unhappy first marriage, according to Harris, he would mope about at home 'for hours by myself reading, brooding, fretting, and even crying bitter tears'.

Finding him in this state, Mary, a handsome but quiet domestic servant, tells him not to 'take on so'. One thing leads to another as it tends to in Harris's accounts and soon Mary is on the sofa with him. But then, disaster.

'A rapid probe, and then my prick! My God! It was not standing, not a bit of swell or stiffness was in it; it was as a sucked gooseberry, a mere bit of dwindling, flexible gristle.'

He goes on to describe his – and to a lesser extent Mary's – efforts to arouse himself to action, but it is all in vain. 'I could not even thumb it up,' he says.

Finally, Mary, being an understanding sort sits up briskly, brushes down her clothes, says, 'I must go and see about laying the things for dinner,' and leaves the room.

For days – and indeed for pages of his book – Harris pursues the maid but, to his growing astonishment and panic, the flesh remains weak. Finally, he makes it (in the book, at least) and cries out at the moment of triumph, 'I've fucked you – I'm a man, you see!'

Mary's response is not recorded.

MOST SEX-STARVED REVOLUTIONARY

In a recent Brazilian bestseller *Alligators and Werewolves*, Herbert Daniel propounds a new form of sexual revolution and casts light on the sex life of urban guerrillas.

Daniel argues that only the promiscuous homosexual is the true revolutionary and refers frequently to the

'Machismo-Leninismo', a phrase which has thrown Brazilian intellectuals into some confusion.

As an ex-revolutionary himself, Daniel is scathing about the sex life of terrorists which is, he claims, almost non-existent. For seven years, he sublimated his sexual needs in the revolution.

Then he went to work in a gay sauna.

CRUELLEST CUT

The most extreme form of circumcision was carried out in the Middle East. As a test of manhood, an Arab father would sometimes demand that, before his son was married, the skin of the entire length of his penis should be removed in front of the victim's bride.

If the boy cried out, he would be regarded as being unworthy of manhood and killed.

GROSSEST FLASHERS

Self exposure is a far from recent phenomenon. Indeed some of the legal records dating from the seventeenth century suggests that in comparison to his historical counterparts, the modern flasher is relatively restrained.

One man, when he found his neighbour's wife 'sitting at work, drawed out his private member and laid it upon her shoulder, and wished that her shoulders was another thing'.

Another 'did take forth his privy parts in his hand and showed the same unto Joan Brown . . . and told her it was a good hard thing, and that she sitting upon a stool he wiped his privy member about her face'.

A similar overture was made by another unrestrained flasher who 'took out his privy member . . . and put the same into her hand, and there made water'.

MOST SPECTACULAR BALLBREAKERS

The most precious part of the male is, in the case of some species, the most valuable. The sex organs of the bristle worm are eaten by the female to aid fertilization. Some types of male squid lose it altogether during mating and, as soon as the male bee penetrates his queen, his penis breaks off and he bleeds to death.

MOST UNUSUAL POSITION

When Eileen Gibson was pushed through the porthole of the liner *Durham Castle* to her death in 1947, the finger of suspicion pointed to James Camb, a steward on the ship.

Camb was certainly with her when she died and a jury found his explanation unconvincing. He claimed

that she had lost consciousness as they made love and he had pushed her through the porthole to revive her.

MOST DELICATE SOCIAL SENSIBILITY

An essential investment for the habitual erotic failure is J. P. Donleavy's invaluable guide *The Unexpurgated Code*.

It contains essential advice over a wide area of questions of etiquette:

Upon Placing the Blame for Venereal Infection Do this as soon as you can and admit to nothing. The first person getting in their accusation stands a better chance of appearing innocent.

Upon Having Without Invitation an Uncontrollable Erection It is extremely bad manners to stand in prolonged postures with your member prominently bulging in front of strange ladies to whom your temporary enormity means little. And to twitch it is a cardinal rudeness.

Solitary Masturbation. Upon coming upon someone engaged in this practice, always demonstrate your broadminded urbanity with a smile and the brief comment, 'Ah, you're in good hands.'

Other trick subjects covered include *Upon Being Stung on the End of Your Prick by a Bee on a Golf Course*, *When the Overwhelming Desire to Goose a Lady Cannot be Suppressed*, *Upon Changing Your Sex* and *The Crab Louse*.

EARLIEST EXAMPLE OF CASTRATION COMPLEX

Mankind has always showed a quite healthy and natural concern to keep womankind's hands off him, except when it suits him. In the days before Y-fronts were invented he was particularly vulnerable.

As a result, the ancient laws show a definite concern with the protection of man's private parts.

In the Old Testament, the Book of Deuteronomy contains the following advice:

'When men fight with one another, and the wife of the one draws near to rescue her husband from the hand of him who is fighting him, and puts out her hand and seizes him by the private parts, then you will cut off her hand.'

And the law of the Assyrians was even more specific:

'If a woman has crushed a man's testicles in an affray, one of her fingers shall be cut off; and if, although the physic has bound it up, the second testicle is affected with it and becomes inflamed of it or if she has crushed the second testicle in the affray, both of her nipples shall be torn off.'

MOST CONCLUSIVE PROOF THAT BLONDES DON'T HAVE MORE FUN

The extraordinary lengths to which males are driven by lack of an outlet for their normal, healthy sexual desires is well illustrated by a rather unkind series of experiments on blond ring doves.

When deprived by a mate, it was discovered that, within a few days, a blond ring dove is prepared to court a white dove that it had previously ignored.

163

After a few more days, it was trying to seduce a stuffed dove. A few more days, a rolled-up cloth was enough to get it going.

Finally the crazed bird would direct its sexual attentions on the empty corner of its cage.

MOST SEXUALLY EXHAUSTED KING

Lion expert Dr Bertram has revealed that the king of the jungle mates an average of 3,000 times for every cat reared to adulthood. When a lioness is in season, the male will mate with her every fifteen minutes or so for several days. Yet, most matings do not result in pregnancy.

LEAST RAMPANT STALLION

When it was revealed in court that Tony Waddington called himself 'The Stallion' and claimed to have fathered twenty-eight children, his ex-lover Lauren Doyle was indignant.

'Tony couldn't father twenty-eight hamsters, let alone twenty-eight children,' she said. 'When we were together, I was lucky to get sex with him once a month. As far as I'm concerned, The Stallion should be put out to pasture.'

The outburst came as Waddington stood accused of stealing a van.

'We used to fight for my vanity mirror,' continued Lauren, 'because Tony likes to wear blusher and mascara.'

LEAST REGAL QUEENS

To avoid erotic failure in the homosexual world, it is important to be able to recognize queens:

The Clean Queen. He does his washing and cruising at the launderette.
The Easter Queen. He comes as quick as a rabbit.
The Dinge Queen. (or Coal Burner) He's white and likes black lovers.
The Midnight Queen. 'You'll never get near him – he's a Midnight Queen and you're not even 7.30.'
The Ribbon Clerk. He has a desk job, and may be found hanging around at the *Vaseline Villa* (YMCA).

MOST INTIMATE CONFESSIONAL

When the vice squad in Turin raided a brothel specializing in 'all over body massage with opportunities for full massage', they found a priest enjoying a particularly heavy meditation session with a thirty-two-year-old Genoese woman.

They later discovered that the establishment was particularly popular among the priesthood.

The password at the door was 'Peace and goodwill'.

MOST EFFECTIVE LOVE CURE

A nineteenth-century American historian, Captain J. G. Bourke, tells the extraordinary story of a man who apparently became obsessed with a prostitute after she had given him a love potion.

Anxious to break the spell, friends of the man managed to get some of her excrement, put it in a new shoe and made him walk in it until he could bear the smell no longer.

When he took the shoe off, he found to his astonishment that he was completely cured.

MOST ELEVATED NIGHTCLUB ACT

The Condor Topless Club, one of the first of its type in the San Francisco Bay area, specialized in unusual stage gimmicks and props, including a piano that could be elevated to the roof. But in November 1983, an unscheduled performance at the club came to a tragic end.

James Ferrozo, the forty-year-old assistant manager, was found one morning fifteen foot up in the air on top of the piano with his twenty-three-year-old girlfriend Theresa Hill. Both of them were naked. She had bruises and a bad hangover; he was dead, having been crushed or asphyxiated as the piano reached the roof of the Condor.

Police speculated that the couple had been involved in an afterhours frolic when the 'Up' button on the piano was accidentally pressed. It took the local fire department three hours to extricate Miss Hill from under Ferrozo's body.

Reporting the tragedy, *Variety* headlined the story: HE DIED HAPPY.

ELEVEN

THE ULTIMATE APHRODISIAC

'I'm never through with a woman
until I've had her three ways.'

John F. Kennedy

SPOOKIEST SPOOK

The legendary director of the FBI, J. Edgar Hoover, was an unusual man.

His forty-eight years at the bureau were marked by a feverish campaign to rid the world of corruption, communism and loose behaviour, although not necessarily in that order.

Hoover used to keep OC (Official and Confidential) files on such prominent figures as Franklin D. Roosevelt, John Kennedy and Martin Luther King in his office. The files were said to concentrate on their sexual behaviour.

He could be said to have had something of an obsession about what he regarded as depravity, remarking on one occasion, 'I regret to say that we of the FBI are powerless to act in cases of oral-genital intimacy, unless it has in some way obstructed inter-state commerce.'

Yet he himself appears to have lived a life of sexual abstinence, although he developed a close friendship with Clyde Tolson, an FBI colleague, to whom he left his entire half-million dollar estate.

But it's most likely that America's sex-obsessed superspook died a virgin.

MOST STRICTLY CONTROLLED MEMBERS

In 1975, the Italian Maoist Party issued a new edict to members.

Henceforth, no maoist should have sex more than once a day.

RANDIEST TAX INSPECTOR

Alfred Ibarura, a French tax inspector, was most conscientious at his job. One day, it occurred to him that there was a professional group in the community who almost certainly were not declaring what they earned – prostitutes.

When he paid an official call on one in Lille, his suspicions were justified. But instead of supplying her with the correct forms, he accepted her offer of a quick one in lieu.

This became something of a habit for Alfred until the unhappy day he tried it on a whore called Roselita who unfortunately did pay her taxes. She reported him to the Inland Revenue.

In court, Alfred admitted blackmailing seventy-five girls into having sex with him. He was fined the equivalent of £75 and jailed for six months.

DUMBEST SOUTH AFRICAN POLICE RAID

When five burly South African policemen broke into the flat of twenty-four-year-old Celeste Cross, they were confident of finding her in bed with an Asian, a heinous crime under the country's Immorality Act.

The case never reached the courts because:

1. Celeste was not in bed.
2. Her boyfriend was not in the flat.
3. He was not Asian but white with a rather heavy suntan.

MOST EASILY FIDDLED EMPEROR

Even by Roman standards, the tastes of Emperor Nero were exotic. A promiscuous seducer and ravisher of men and women (probably in that order) he had distinctly sadistic leanings.

At one of his frequent orgies, he first raped a Vestal Virgin and then castrated one of his male favourites, a man called Sporus, 'even endeavouring to transform him into a woman', according to historian Suetonius.

Later he went through a form of marriage with Sporus, and would take him around Solemu assemblies dressed like an empress, 'kissing from time to time as they rode together'.

Not all Nero's endeavours ended so happily. Early in his reign, he would disguise himself as a slave and lurk around the squalid quarters of Rome, among the brothels and wine shops, stealing and sexually assaulting men and women.

At first, he received considerable physical and mental abuse but then word got out that this was one of the Emperor's pranks and that to resist him meant a certain death penalty.

An unprecedented crime wave broke out in the back streets of Rome.

Later in his life, Nero's tastes became more exotic. He devised a game in which, covered by the skin of a wild animal, he would be let loose from a cage into a room where men and women were tied to stakes. He would then savage their private parts.

Once satisfied, the gored victims would be despatched by Doryphorus, Nero's henchman (and, of course, lover).

BEST SOUTH AFRICAN POLICE ALIBI

A white police constable discovered making love to a fifteen-year-old black girl in a funeral parlour in Johannesburg had the perfect alibi. He was searching the girl for drugs.

Impressed by the policeman's rigorous attention to duty, the court was particularly lenient, letting him go with a six-month suspended jail sentence.

LEAST SUCCESSFUL MENAGE À TROIS

In the eleventh century, Count Gulielmas took pleasure in seeing his pet ape make love to his wife.

The unusual arrangement was broken up when the ape, seeing the Count making love to the Countess, was overcome by jealousy and attacked and killed him.

CREEPIEST KING'S SUBJECT

In order to avoid temptation while travelling with the queen of Syria on a long journey, a young nobleman called Cambobus castrated himself. Then, before leaving, he presented to the king an ornate sealed casket.

During the journey, the queen attempted to seduce Cambobus, and when rumours reached the ear of the king, he was arrested and charged with adultery.

But Cambobus was not finished. The king was asked

to open the casket, and there lay the case for the defence – the accused man's testicles.

MOST UNUSUAL THERAPY

A court in Bad Boll, Germany accepted the argument of the defendant Dr Schuetze that having sexual intercourse with his patients was sometimes an important part of their treatment.

However they were concerned to hear that a sixteen-year-old girl had found the doctor's therapy pleasurable because this contravened medical ethics.

The court concluded that in future such treatment must take place in the presence of a medical assistant while, in the case of teenagers, parental permission must be obtained.

MOST IMPOSSIBLE REGAL REQUEST

Cotys, the King of Thrace, was a pleasure-loving but prickly individual. A lover of great, orgiastic banquets, his most famous celebration was on the day, according to the king, the goddess Athena was to marry him.

At the height of the drunken revels, Cotys despatched a messenger to a specially constructed bridal chamber to see whether the goddess had arrived. When the unfortunate messenger returned with the news that there was no one in the chamber, the king shot him dead with a bow.

A second messenger was sent off but was killed for the same reason. Rather more intelligently, the third messenger reported that Athena was now awaiting her new husband.

History does not relate how Cotys fared with his deific bride but one can safely assume that she pleased him more than a later wife. In a fit of jealousy, he cut her up, starting with the pudenda.

MOST PREMATURE RELIGIOUS LEADER

The late Aly Khan suffered seriously from premature ejaculation until he found a stylish solution to his problem.

He would keep a champagne ice bucket by his bed into which he'd plunge his hand at the moment of crisis.

NARROWEST KNOWN ESCAPE FOR AN MP

When *Ruling Passions*, Tom Driberg's graphic account of his life in politics, society and public lavatories was published after his death, there was surprise among his parliamentary colleagues. They all knew that he liked a bit of rough but few realized how relentless his pursuit of working-class boys was.

He claims that, if anything, his promiscuity became more pronounced after he became an MP. It was during this period that he had two narrow escapes.

The first actually reached the courts but was hushed up by his friends on Fleet Street. Returning home one night, Driberg came across two miners who were looking for a place to spend the night. Anxious, as he later explained, to use them for research on behalf of the *Daily Express*, he invited them home. Various 'dormitory permutations' were proposed but in the end all three of them ended up in Driberg's bed. In the middle of the night, they both leapt up and quite unreasonably accused him of trying to seduce them.

When the case came to court, he was found not guilty.

On another occasion, Driberg was taking time off from canvassing for a by-election in Edinburgh, when he picked up, or was picked up by, a 'flaxen-haired and smilingly attractive' Norwegian sailor. They repaired to the local public lavatory where, as Driberg puts it, 'I was soon on my knees.'

At that moment, a young Scottish policeman walked in and, seeing the scene, said, 'Och, ye bastards – ye dirty pair o' whoors!'

But Driberg remained calm. As the Norwegian adjusted his dress, he stood up to confront the policeman and explained who he was – an MP and writer of the William Hickey column in the *Daily Express*.

'William Hickey!' exclaimed the man. 'Good God, man, I've read ye all of my life! Every morning!'

Soon the two were in deep conversation and the policeman took the incident in the 'cottage' no further. Driberg even managed to restrain himself for a few moments, later writing that he 'judged that it would be going too far, in the circumstances, to make a pass'.

MOST UNDIGNIFIED EXIT

Felix Fauré experienced a fatal erotic failure in 1899. He was said to have suffered a massive coronary while enjoying a specially designed 'sex chair'.

GAYEST ROMAN EMPEROR

Although less well known than such distinguished erotic failures as Nero and Caligula, Heliogabalus has a strong claim to being Rome's weirdest Emperor.

Heliogabalus, like most of his fellow emperors, covered most perversions in his time but spectacular self-disgust and masochism were his speciality.

Early in his reign, he behaved in a more or less conventional way. He worshipped Baal at a temple flanked by two colossal phalli. He wore female clothes. While celebrating the rites of his deity, he would throw on to a great fire the severed genitals of pubescent boys, and so on.

But then he started going off the rails. He toyed with the idea of castrating himself and tried unsuccessfully to convince his physicians to turn him into a woman. He finally settled on circumcision.

He fantasized that he was a particularly lewd woman and would go out of his way to get caught by his 'husband' and punished severely.

Then he would go out at night to a brothel, drive out the prostitutes and, wearing a wig, solicit trade from passers-by.

Finally the Roman army and people grew tired of his behaviour. Heliogabalus was murdered with the

rest of his household and his body was thrown into the Tiber.

LEAST SUCCESSFUL SATANIC SACRIFICE

Not all the excesses of 'the Great Beast' Aleister Crowley were successes – as Crowley's lieutenant Raoul Loveday was to discover.

Loveday had fallen under Crowley's spell and had taken his young wife Betty May to Italy to join his notorious abbey in Sicily.

Never truly at home among the 'unspeakably vile things' that took place here, Betty – now called Sister Sybilline – decided to cut and run the day that Crowley calmly announced, 'We shall sacrifice Sister Sybilline at eight o'clock tonight.' She escaped that day and hid in the mountains near the abbey.

Frustrated by her disappearance, the Great Beast turned his attentions to an unlucky cat. Having hypnotized it, he put it in a bag. Crowley's current scarlet woman held a cup in which to catch the blood. The privilege of acting as executioner was to be Loveday's.

Unfortunately the occasion (and possibly a cocktail of drugs) proved too much for him and he stabbed the bag lightly and ineffectually. The cat ran bleeding and yowling around the room until it was recaptured and sacrificed in a more efficient way. The precious blood was caught in the cup and Loveday dutifully drank it.

A few days later he went down with enteric fever, which was almost certainly contracted from the cat's blood. His mentor Crowley predicted he would die on 16 February, which he duly did.

Betty returned to England and sold her story to the *Sunday Express*.

MOST OVER-RATED ROMANCE

They called it the Romance of the Century. He was King of England; she was twice married and known in society as 'an adventuress'. Yet the truth about Edward VIII and Wallis Simpson may have been rather different.

In *Duchess*, his biography of Mrs Simpson, Stephen Birmingham advances the theory that their relationship was largely asexual.

'Lord Castlerosse, who knew the Prince (Edward) well, insisted that the attraction between the two was not primarily sexual. In fact, throughout Wallis's courtship period, no one saw them so much as kiss . . . Wallis herself dismissed sex as the main source of attraction.'

Birmingham concludes that neither of them was particularly interested in physical love. Wallis Simpson once confessed, 'I have had two husbands, and I never went to bed with either of them.'

As for Edward, his first wife had complained that he suffered from a chronic problem of premature ejaculation. One of his friends went further.

'To put it bluntly,' he said, 'he had the smallest pecker I have ever seen.'

LEAST SATISFACTORY MINISTERIAL
PERFORMANCE

Later to be at the centre of a more spectacular erotic failure, Tory ex-minister Cecil Parkinson survived an unpleasant moment during a House of Commons debate.

Then Industry Secretary, Parkinson was addressing the House with a statesmanlike hand in the pocket when there was an interruption from a member of Her Majesty's Opposition.

'Stop playing with yourself,' shouted loud-mouthed Labour MP Dennis Skinner.

'I couldn't leave my hand in,' Parkinson later explained to friends, 'and I couldn't take it out because it would have looked as if I'd been doing what he said. So I froze for thirty seconds.'

BUSIEST EMPEROR

Although Napoleon won as many victories off the field of battle as on it, his life was not without a variety of erotic failures.

Excessively timid towards women, he made a habit in his early life of proposing to women considerably more mature than him. Two of them were Madame de Montansier (aged 60) and Madame Perron (aged 40).

When he finally married the famous Josephine de Beauharnais, their wedding night ended in disaster. As Napoleon made love to his new wife, her pet pug, believing his mistress was being attacked, leapt on to the bed and bit the general hard on his left buttock.

In fact, buttocks played an important part in Napoleon's private life. In 1798, he became smitten with the young wife of one of his lieutenants who had dressed up in male attire to be with her husband. Enrolled as his mistress, she would wear skintight white pantaloons that would appeal to his buttock fetish.

The theory that the emperor swung both ways has never been proved. He tolerated and possibly encouraged homosexuality among his soldiers, and would often choose aides who were particularly effeminate looking. The emperor's personal orderly actually used to refer to him as 'Her Majesty'.

After his marriage to Josephine was annulled in 1809, Napoleon sought a second wife, finally settling on Marie Louise of Austria, an eighteen-year-old virgin so pure that, during her childhood, all male animals were kept from her view. With certain lack of Gallic charm, the emperor said that she had 'the kind of womb I want to marry'.

Meanwhile his liaisons continued. His affair with Maria Walewska began badly when, on their first night together, she fainted during foreplay. Napoleon proceeded to rape her.

It was said at the time that Maria had passed out as a result of sexual aggressiveness on the part of her lover, but it might have been shock. A medical examination after he had died revealed that the emperor, now ravaged by disease, was less than well-endowed.

One inch, to be precise.

STRONGEST CASE FOR SCALPING

When King Menephta of Egypt defeated the Libyans in battle around 1300 BC, it was recorded on a monument that over 13,000 phalluses were brought home as victory tokens.

Broken down by rank and nationality, the score read:

Libyan generals	6
Libyan other ranks	6356
Sirculians	222
Etruscans	542
Greeks	6111

Apparently, after the battle, these trophies were presented to the king.

FUSSIEST BILLIONAIRE

Everything Howard Hughes did, whether it was making money, taking over Hollywood or going mad, he did with total thoroughness. His attention to his sex life was similarly meticulous.

For thirty years, he pursued – and, being Howard Hughes, most often caught – a number of Hollywood stars. Among the actresses associated with him during this period were Katherine Hepburn, Hedy Lamarr, Jean Harlow, Ava Gardner and Carole Lombard. Although he paid particular attention to Jane Russell's career – and for one film actually designed a bra for her – they never became lovers.

Another failure was Gina Lollobrigida who, as a young actress, was invited to come to Hollywood.

When she found that she was a virtual prisoner under twenty-four-hour guard and that Howard Hughes was part of a package, she fled.

Unsatisfied by his star lovers, Hughes set up a network of detectives to procure girls for him. They would comb the country for beautiful young things, promise them a screen test in Hollywood and, if Hughes accepted them, set them up in Los Angeles. At one stage, he had five houses around the town with a different starlet in each waiting for him to pop in.

Not that this operation was without its tricky moments. On one occasion, Hughes was making love to one of his harem, a fifteen-year-old from North Carolina, when her mother broke into the room. Hughes paid up $250,000 to avoid statutory rape charges.

But what qualifies Hughes as an erotic failure is the turn his sex life took in the early 1960s when, despite being supplied with some of America's most beautiful women, he decided to give up sex. Now obsessed with a fear of germs, he decided to avoid any physical contact that might pass them over to him.

He took up drugs and watching twenty-four-hour television instead.

TWELVE

EXPERTS' CORNER

'Little attention was paid to the female orgasm before the era of sexology. Where did the sexologists find it? Did they discover it or invent it? Or both?'

Dr Leslie H. Farber

MOST INACTIVE AMERICAN LOVERS

A recent survey by New York University's sleep disorders centre has found that more than five million Americans habitually fall asleep while making love.

The report did not reveal whether their partners noticed any difference in their performance.

LEAST FASHIONABLE FORMULA FOR INCREASING LINGAM SIZE

According to Wu Hsien, a Taoist Master of the Han Dynasty, men with disappointingly small organs, or *lingams*, need not despair.

'There is a way to enlarge an unusually small weapon. In the early hours of the morning, when the Yin-force is diminishing and the Yang-force is increasing, the man should face East and meditate calmly. He should breathe deeply forty-nine times, drawing breath from his abdomen. Then he should rub the palms of his hands together until they are scorching hot. Next he should hold his weapon with his right hand, concentrate his mind, and with his left hand he should rub his navel centre, encircling it to the left for eighty-one rotations. He then switches hands, rubbing his navel centre in the same way, but encircling to the right for eighty-one times. He then should roll his weapon between his hands, as if making a thread from fibres.'

Works every time, they say.

MOST DISASTROUSLY EFFECTIVE CURSE

When a Kenyan woman who suspected her husband of infidelity asked the local witchdoctor to cast a spell on him, she had no idea quite how effective it would be.

The next day, the husband was rushed to hospital, locked painfully and inextricably together with his lover. It took doctors six hours to prise the unhappy couple apart.

UNFRIENDLIEST FEMINIST

Valerie Solanas was, it is generally agreed, on the radical wing of the new feminism of the 1970s. She set up a group called S.C.U.M. – the Society for Cutting Up Men – and included in her manifesto this description of the enemy:

'The male is an incomplete female, a walking abortion, aborted at the gene stage. To be male is to be deficient, emotionally crippled: maleness is a deficiency disease and males are emotional cripples.'

Valerie later achieved some notoriety for shooting walking abortion Andy Warhol in the stomach.

LEAST KNOWN AUSTRALIAN
CONTRACEPTIVE METHOD

In 1928, a letter from an Australian to Marie Stopes revealed a popular form of contraception among the aborigines.

'Their method is to make an insertion in the male organ, underneath, near junction with the body. This cut is healed much the same as perforation with ear-ring. They can fulfil all obligations except propagate; as the seed is passed out at the perforation. We call them whistle-cocks.'

WORST NEWS FOR MRS BELKIN

In the Russian magazine *Health*, Dr Belkin, an expert in such matters, has ruled that the correct duration for sexual intercourse is precisely two minutes.

LEAST INTERESTING SEXUAL THEORY

Dr Ivor Felstein has revealed a sure symptom of erotic failure – a tendency to yawn. Those who yawn, he says, are usually sexually immature or suffer from a 'low sexual tension, with frequent failure to be aroused'.

Reactions to the doctor's theory have shown an astonishingly high incidence of sexual immaturity and low sexual tension among his readers.

MOST COMPLEX SEXUAL USE
FOR HYDRAULICS

Impotent men in America are being helped by a new device, pioneered by Professor F. Brantley Scott of Baylor University College of Medicine.

It consists of two balloonlike cylinders which are inserted in the penis. The cylinders are connected by tubing to a small reservoir of blood behind the abdominal wall which in its turn is connected to a pump in the scrotal sack.

A quick manipulation of the pump produces an instant erection and a release valve on the pump deflates it.

By 1980, 1500 patients were using Professor Scott's self-pumper. The operation costs $9000.

LEAST STIMULATING LOVE POTION

John McGill of Harmony Sex Aids claimed that their love potion 'Span-Fly' was guaranteed to turn on any man or woman.

When a customer, having paid £3 for six packets, discovered that all it stimulated was a bad case of wind, the police were called in. Tests proved that 'Span-Fly' contained no more than caffeine, citric acid and bicarbonate of soda.

McGill was fined £300.

SILLIEST SURVEY

After ten years' research, Professor Nancy Hirshberg of the University of Illinois, wrote a major paper on what kind of men are attracted to what kind of physical features of a woman.

Her main findings were:

1. Men who like women with big breasts tend to be outgoing, independent and selfish.
2. Women with big buttocks are guilty, introverted and socially ill at ease.
3. Sociable men prefer women with nice legs.
4. Women with nice legs are above all concerned with making a good impression.

When asked the significance of all this, Professor Hirshberg said, 'I don't know.'

CHEAPEST ARTIFICIAL LIMB

After his application, supported by several doctors, was passed 'at high level' in the Ministry of Health, a man who was paralysed from the waist downwards was supplied with an artificial penis on the National Health.

'The psychological effect was fantastic,' said his wife. 'It has made a new man of him.'

It cost £15.

STRONGEST REASONS FOR GRATITUDE TO THE LONDON RUBBER COMPANY

A wide variety of unappetizing contraceptives were used in our early history. A bung of crocodile or elephant dung was popular in some countries up until the thirteenth century.

The Roman writer Pliny also provided helpful advice on the subject. He recommended mouse dung applied in the form of a lineament, swallowing snail excrement, or pigeon's droppings mixed with oil and wine.

Alternatively you could hide the blood and testicles of a cock under the bed.

But there was nothing, Pliny concluded, to beat rubbing a woman's loins with the blood taken from the ticks on a wild black bull. This would generally lead to the best possible contraceptive system – a total aversion to sex.

MOST ENTERPRISING CONTRIBUTION TO THE EXPORT DRIVE

Farmers in the Isle of Man were reported in 1980 to have responded well to an unusual demand from the Far East. Dealers in Hong Kong were buying up the gall-stones of slaughtered Manx cattle for £30 an ounce to sell as an aphrodisiac.

LEAST DIGNIFIED EXIT

In Bavaria, a man was reported to have met an untimely death as a result of his penchant for an electric potato masher.

With fiendish ingenuity, he had adapted the contraption to give a very special thrill when he plugged it into a light socket.

But while indulging himself with the masher while sitting on the lavatory (no, the report did not reveal where the lavatory fitted in), the man made a fatal mistake. He touched the chain, earthed himself and was electrocuted on the spot.

Yet another great invention with a fatal flaw.

MOST DRASTIC WAYS OF
AVOIDING PREMATURE BLINDNESS

Masturbation has always been a source of worry for some people. In the Egyptian *Book of the Dead* it is condemned and, in early Jewish history, it was sometimes punished by execution.

In the eighteenth and nineteenth century, abusing the self-abuser became more feverish with such scientific works as *Onania, or the Heinous Sin of Self Pollution, Eronania and Spermatorrhea* being published.

Since it was now generally accepted that masturbation caused fevers, lassitude, epilepsy, insanity, melancholia, decay of the spinal chord and paralysis, almost certainly ending in suicide, much attention was paid to ways of suppressing the evil.

J. L. Milton, the author of *Spermatorrhea*, describes specially designed cages with spikes which parents

195

could use on a dangerously pubescent son. At the first hint of an erection, the device would ring a bell in the parental bedroom.

Warming to his theme, Milton also suggested blistering the penis with red mercury ointment.

This was a mild cure compared to that practised on a man in Texas later in the nineteenth century. There they decided to avoid half-measures and amputated the whole thing.

LEAST APPETIZING APHRODISIAC

In the hope of regenerating their sex organs, Chinese eunuchs were in the habit of eating the still-warm brains of decapitated animals.

LEAST IMPRESSIVE PARTICULARS

The smallest male organ discovered by Kinsey was one inch long, but there are medical reports of what doctors sometimes refer to as 'the micropenis', whose length is no more than one centimetre.

Not, of course, that size is relevant in any way.

STRONGEST ARGUMENTS FOR IMPOTENCE

Research into male impotence continues apace in laboratories all around the world. Several breakthroughs have recently been announced.

In Rumania, a plastic device can be implanted in the area of the groin.

In America, blood circulation in the penis can be improved by a surgical operation transplanting stomach arteries.

Luckiest of all are the French. There, Professor Louis Subrini has perfected a device for inserting silicone cylinders into the male member to produce an instant erection.

How you get it to go down is not explained.

LEAST SUCCESSFUL AUSTRALIAN MEDICAL BREAKTHROUGH

Sales of a new male contraceptive pill fell off dramatically after men started losing their hair having taken it.

Dr Stan White of Sidney University reported that the manufacturers were not worried.

'Their pill can be employed in chemical sheep shearing,' he said.

LEAST GRATEFUL PATIENT

In a recent operation in Salisbury, Rhodesia, Mr George Least was given a second heart to support his own.

While recovering, he shot himself for love of a nurse who was looking after him.

WORST CONTROLLED PARANORMAL EXPERIMENT

A recent conference entitled 'Is Anything There?' was told of the case of a woman who, like Uri Geller, could bend metal using psychic powers.

She was unfortunately out of action at present – during an experiment, her contraceptive coil had accidentally warped and she was pregnant.

MOST PAINFUL SELF-IMPROVEMENT COURSE

A revolutionary surgical technique has been introduced by a doctor in Japan. Grafting muscle from the buttocks, he can build up the end of his patients' penis to impressive proportions.

LEAST APPEALING CURE FOR IMPOTENCE

The good news is that Dr Leonard Sacks of Los Angeles has come up with what he claims is a remedy for impotency. The bad news is that it involves putting a staple through your ear with a surgical gun normally used for doing incisions after operations.

The doctor claiming that the staple made obese patients feel full when they rubbed it. It also made them feel randy. His researches started there.

LEAST CONVINCING ARGUMENT FOR NUCLEAR POWER

Top American Nuclear Scientist Dr Edward Teller once told *US* magazine that a young couple in bed can receive from potassium in the blood as much radioactivity from one another as they would from leaning against a nuclear power station.

MOST DANGEROUS CLAPTRAP

A recent international survey reveals that prostitutes are no longer the major communicators of VD. The list of most likely carriers goes:

1. Airline staff
2. Tourists
3. Lorry drivers
4. Servicemen

OHIO'S BIGGEST GYNAECOLOGICAL BREAKTHROUGH

A gynaecologist in Ohio has proposed a course of surgery that will transform the lives of millions of women who are only, as he puts it, 'randomly vaginally orgasmic'.

Dr James Burt's technique is simple: reconstruct the vagina so that the clitoris is 'more accessible to direct penile stimulation'.

A report in *World Medical News* reveals that Dr Burt has carried out the operation on 4,000 women, including his lovely lady wife Joan who, according to the doctor, is 'demonstrable proof of his claim' that, after the operation, women have more frequent and more intense orgasms than before.

The exact new location of the clitoris was not revealed.

MOST INNOVATIVE LADYCARE CLINIC

Ladycare Private Pregnancy and Information Service
of Ealing offered a wide range of services of a personal
kind, even including a revolutionary abortion technique.

Alerted to their activities, the ever-vigilant *Sunday
People* sent a woman reporter round to investigate the
clinic. In true Sunday paper tradition, the woman
pretended to be 'in trouble'.

Thomas Pond, the manager of the clinic, explained
his special abortion service. It was, he said, a medically
proven fact that, in the early stages of pregnancy, a
prolonged sexual climax will cause a miscarriage. As
part of the clinic's personal service, he was prepared to
induce this with the help of a vibrator. So if she would
just slip out of her –

The reporter made her excuses and left.

SELECTED BIBLIOGRAPHY

A. Alvarez, *Life After Marriage* (Macmillan, 1982)

Kenneth Anger, *Hollywood Babylon* (Dell, 1975)

Ivan Bloch, *Sexual Life in England* (Arco, 1958)

Peter Bowler and Jonathon Green, *What a Way to Go* (Pan, 1983)

E. J. Burford, *The Orrible Synne* (Calder and Boyars, 1973)

Alex Comfort, *The Anxiety Makers* (Nelson, 1967)

Armand Denis, *Taboo* (W. H. Allen, 1966)

J. P. Donleavy, *The Unexpurgated Code* (Wildwood House, 1975)

Nik Douglas and Penny Slinger, *Sexual Secrets* (Hutchinson, 1979)

Tom Driberg, *Ruling Passions* (Jonathan Cape, 1977)

I. L. C. Fergusson, *Records and Curiosities in Obstetrics and Gynaecology* (Bailliere Tindall, 1982)

Ian Gibson, *The English Vice* (Duckworth, 1978)

Ruth Hall (Ed.), *Dear Marie Stopes* (Andre Deutsch, 1978)

Shere Hite, *Hite Report: Nationwide Study of Female Sexuality* (Corgi, 1981); *Hite Report: Study of Male Sexuality* (Macdonald, 1981)

B. S. Johnson (Ed.), *You Always Remember The First Time* (Quartet, 1975)

Hugh Kingsmill, *Made in Heaven* (Hamish Hamilton, 1937)

John Knowler, *Trust an Englishman* (Jonathan Cape, 1972)

Christopher Logue, *Bumper Book of True Stories* (Private Eye, 1980)

Konrad Lorenz, *On Aggression* (Methuen, 1966)

Linda Lovelace *Ordeal* (W. H. Allen, 1980)

Steven Marcus, *The Other Victorians* (Weidenfeld, 1966)

Bob Monkhouse, *The Book of Days* (Arrow, 1981)

Richard Neville, *Playpower* (Jonathan Cape, 1970)

Barry Norman, *The Hollywood Greats* (Hodder & Stoughton, 1980)

Burgo Partridge, *A History of Orgies* (Spring Books, 1966)

Punch, *Cuttings 1, 2 and 3* (Elm Tree, 1980, 1981, 1983)

G. R. Quaife, *Wanton Wenches and Wayward Wives* (Croom Helm, 1979)

Marian Roalfe Cox, *An Introduction to Folk-Lore* (David Nutt, 1904)

G. L. Simons, *The Book of World Sexual Records* (Corgi, 1983)

Janet Street-Porter, *Scandal!* (Elm Tree, 1981)

Marie Stopes, *Enduring Passion* (Putnam, 1928)

Lawrence Stone, *The Family, Sex and Marriage: England 1500–1800* (Weidenfeld & Nicolson, 1977)

Thomas Szasz, *Sex: Facts, Frauds and Fallacies* (Blackwell, 1980)

Reay Tannahill, *Sex in History* (Hamish Hamilton, 1980)

Wallace, Wallace, Wallechinsky and Wallace, *The Intimate Sex Lives of Famous People* (Hutchinson, 1981)

Stephen Winkworth, *Amazing Times* (Allen and Unwin, 1983)

Wayland Young, *Eros Denied* (Weidenfeld and Nicolson, 1965)

THE BOOK OF HEROIC FAILURES

Stephen Pile

'Are you fed up with all these books telling you how to be a success? Are you dreadful at most things you try? Here at long last is a book in praise of spectacular failures and people who can't do a thing'
Namib Times

'One of the few books to make me laugh out loud'
Sunday Express

'One of the funniest and most entertaining books I have dipped into for a long time'
Country Life

'(A) splendid panorama of non-achievement'
Sunday Telegraph

'As a serious book it's a failure, as a tonic to make your ribs ache, it's a rip-roaring success'
Manchester Evening News

'A disaster'
STEPHEN PILE

Futura Publications
Non Fiction
0 7088 1908 7

THE BOOK OF MISTAIKES

Gyles Brandreth

'English shorthand typist. Efficien. Useless. Apply otherwise.'
ADVERTISEMENT IN A SPANISH NEWSPAPER

'The ladies of St Martin's Church have discarded clothing of all kinds. Call at 152 North Street for inspection. Mrs Freeman will be willing to oblige you in any way she can.'
Worthing Gazette

'On making enquiries at the Hospital this afternoon, we learn that the deceased is as well as can be expected.'
Jersey Evening Post

THE BOOK OF MISTAIKES

An amazing mixture of misprints, misnomers and misunderstandings . . . a collection of classic clangers, hilarious howlers and headlines gone haywire . . . a dictionary of disaster ranging from the decidedly dreadful to the definitely delightful.

Futura Publications
Humour
0 7088 2194 4

HOW TO BE A WALLY

Paul Manning

HOW TO BE A WALLY
in the comfort of your own home! Yes! With the help
of easy, step-by-step diagrams, you can learn how
to:

Stand outside DER showrooms in the rain watching
'Game For a Laugh'
Feed prawn-cocktail flavour crisps to the lions in
safari parks
Get the best out of your Colonel Bogey car horn
Destroy a Spanish football stadium

   plus much more besides!

HOW TO BE A WALLY
The complete, no holds-barred guide to the wally
lifestyle – *at a price you can afford*!

Futura Publications
Non-Fiction/Humour
0 7088 2440 4